The Hungry Horse

By JK Worth

Copyright © 2024 by JK Worth.

Disclaimer

Any references to real people, events, locales, establishments or organizations are solely intended to provide a sense of authenticity, and as such are used fictionally. All names, all characters, incidents and dialogue are the author's creation and should not be considered real.

Table of Contents

1954

Every town in America that has a hydroelectric plant seems to have a similar sign. The people living in Hungry Horse, Montana, just didn't know exactly what "Best Dam Town" meant yet. Somebody knew what made it a good place when it was painted on a four-by-eight sheet of plywood and erected on Highway 2, just outside of town. The cute but "naughty" sign, by 1954 standards, didn't provide a clue as to why they liked living there—they just did. Things were different back then; a lot slower, it seemed, and certainly much simpler.

The citizens of Hungry Horse didn't know that one day, not only would everything be turned upside down, but it would happen twice in their generation. It would take them all by surprise. For now though, things were looking rosy.

Having a new hydroelectric power plant in your town meant one thing—cheap electricity—and with it, hopefully, a lot of good jobs. Thanks to geography, Hungry Horse would get them both. The first to come were the loggers. Flooding 22,500 acres of Montana wilderness for a 34-mile-long reservoir and the fourth largest concrete dam in the world would make over ninety million board feet of timber available for the rest of the country. Twelve companies and three thousand men and women working under a $43 million bid, completed the project in less than 1500 days—500 days sooner than the contract called for. Part of the Columbia River System; it was the pride of the state.

In 1954, forest management was a euphemism for cutting down trees. Clearcutting without replanting was considered normal, but things were changing, and some of the more forward-thinking companies were planting seedlings for future harvests. Since the land would be totally covered with water, they would take every tree below the waterline. When you don't have to worry about reclamation or public relations, the job is pretty simple: cut down as many trees as possible in the shortest amount of time. And that's just what they did.

These sawyers outdid Paul Bunyan on a good day. Instead of using saws, they used steel cable and eight-foot iron balls made of three-quarter-inch steel plates and a couple of huge diesel-powered tractors. The four-and-a-half-ton steel balls were used to get the cable up off the ground to avoid catching stumps. The additional height also generated more leverage. It worked by circling the timber with the cable and then slowly winching it in. The cable would slice through trees up to four feet thick, snapping them off at ground level as the tractors reeled in the cable. These men would surround five acres of timber at a time and lay it down on the ground in no time at all. Loading them into trucks and getting them to the local mills and to the railroad was the hardest part.

The Great Northern Railroad delivered the timber from Seattle to Chicago and the places in between located along the northern 'main line.'

The news about the new aluminum plant spread through town faster than the winter winds that rip through Bad Rock Canyon. Small tracts of land in the town were bought and sold by speculators who made money before the business and architectural plans for the new plant were even dry. Cheap electricity, the Great Northern Railroad and the ore in the ground brought the new mining company here. It was the perfect marriage. Aluminum production requires a lot of energy—energy that the Hungry Horse River could provide. The hydroelectric plant was coming on line soon, and now the promise of the 'American Dream' was within reach for over 700 people, and soon the dream would become reality. The plant site was a beautiful landscape scene located on the middle fork of the Hungry Horse River, with Teakettle Mountain as its backdrop. The pastoral setting would soon be gone, exchanged for a factory and a promise for the future. The site and the mines covered almost three square miles. Teakettle Mountain would be hollowed out for its ore. As long as the minerals held out, the workers could expect a decent job and, based upon conservative projections, their grandkids would have jobs too, if they wanted them.

The name Hungry Horse was given to a lake, river, mountain and now a dam. It was thought to be Indian in origin, but old timers knew the real story. There were actually two hungry horses, Tex and Jerry. During the winter of 1900-1901, Bill Prindeville of nearby LaSalle was 'freighting' up two horses laden with well-drilling casing. He suspected there was oil in an area now known as Glacier National Park. On the two-day trip back down, the horses wandered off from the sleighs at night. They were missing for over a month in belly-deep snow. When Bill found them, they were emaciated and living on nothing but willow branches and the brush that broke through the snow. He packed in oats and fed them for days to get their strength up for the trip out. The first night out, Bill stopped at a ranch and the hands all came out to look at the 'hungry horses.' From that day forward, the area was known as Hungry Horse.

Fifty-four years after old Tex and Jerry were rescued, a portable office was set up in town for interviewing prospective employees. It was brought in on a large trailer and had four private interview rooms, with a small seating area by the main door. No one saw it when it was delivered; it just showed up one day out of nowhere. The townspeople slowed down as they drove past it and looked at the door as if it were the gateway to something better. Everyone would have liked it more if it didn't have those wheels under it. After all, it seemed to sneak in when no one was looking and therefore, most assumed that it could sneak out the same way. There was no word about when the interviews would begin. The office on wheels just sat there, silently raising expectations, as its tires sank lower into the Spring mud.

The real estate market was like a game of Monopoly. People were rolling the dice and making their moves. Seventy families that had virtually nothing to their names but a tract of land in the middle of nowhere had now become rich. Lumbering their land, selling the timber and then selling the property to the government for the dam made them the town's nouveau riche. It soon became apparent that two classes of people were forming in Hungry Horse. Most of the population would be working at the plant, and the others would receive a windfall from the land that they owned. They would then make more money from real estate deals, construction projects and eventually from the future employees of the new mine and aluminum plant. The workers would be happy to exchange their pay for the things they needed and wanted, while the store owners and the landlords would be just as happy to take them up on it.

The new operation would be called The Glacier Mining Company. It was a privately held, family-owned business, and the family intended to keep it that way. The Lindstrom family was from Butte and had made a small fortune mining copper in the late 40s.

Three brothers were equal partners with unequal visions. John, the oldest at 32, was a geologist and was as good as anyone at using science to 'look' under the ground or inside a mountain to discover what minerals were hidden there. John had a sixth sense, and he knew it. Every time he selected a site, it paid off in spades. He was almost never wrong and always mentioned it. This venture, and Teakettle Mountain, had something more in it than aluminum, and John was certain about that. For the time being, though, he wasn't revealing what his instincts were telling him; not even to his own brothers. He would save this one for later and gain the greater glory then.

Michael, at 30, was the financial wizard. He could always find backers for any of their projects. A string of successes made that task a lot easier, but the way in which he would structure a deal was a work of art. And, just as artwork becomes more valuable with age, so would Michael's deals. He just seemed to squeeze every drop out of a contract. Most of the brilliance of the deals wouldn't become apparent until months later, and this gave him a solid reputation as an incredible negotiator. It also gave him a large ego.

Brad was the salesman in the family and also the baby at 24. Everything he touched turned to gold, it seemed. He lived for the sale. It didn't matter what it was as long as he sold it. As a kid, he cut lawns in the summer and sold Christmas cards door to door in the frigid autumns of Montana. The cold weather didn't bother him at all. He would trudge through Butte selling engraved cards for three weeks until he made enough money to buy a new bike or whatever else was on his list. He shoveled snow in the winter and never missed waking up early after a late-night snowfall so that he could get all his work done before school. He got any job he wanted because he was so incredibly dependable for a young schoolboy.

His secret to waking up during a late-night snowstorm was a flash of ingenuity that John and Brad came up with together. Brad would set a tray of salt outside his bedroom window with two wires connected at opposite sides of the tray. The wires were attached to a six-volt battery and to a small electric buzzer in his bedroom. When it snowed, the flakes would melt on the salt, and the liquid would complete an electric circuit. The wires were slightly raised from the bottom of the tray, calibrated to sound the alarm only if more than two inches of new snow fell.

In college, he sold almost everything, from ladies' shoes to men's suits. Brad always worked on commission without any salary; he wouldn't have it any other way. Higher risks meant higher gains. He was able to cover all his expenses by working sixteen hours a week. When he worked more, he made a lot of money. He earned a degree in mathematics but decided that the math profession wasn't for him. This decision when reached when Brad, not even working full time his senior year, was making more money than his mathematics professors.

Brad sold the finished metals for the mining company, and since he was good and was on commission, he was the highest-paid employee—something of which the other brothers always took notice. As far as he was concerned, that's the way it should be. To Brad, the salesman is the lifeblood of any company. Brad's attitude was pretty basic. He felt that everyone in the company 'worked' for the salesman, and if he couldn't get that kind of cooperation, how could he serve his customers properly?

Soon, the Lindstrom boys would be 'honoring' Hungry Horse with their presence. This was their biggest venture yet, and they funded the entire project with personal loans and their own capital. John, Michael and Brad would be moving to town.

The Plant

The new aluminum plant was nearing completion, and finally, the process of hiring workers had begun. The new dam and hydroelectric facility was on line and was a thing of beauty. It had been over fourteen months since that portable office had been wheeled into town. Some people thought this day would never come; others thought it was a cruel tease to put that portable office in such a conspicuous place so far in advance of the actual interviewing and hiring process. People likened it to kids waiting for Christmas to come and looking under the Christmas tree at all the nicely wrapped gifts that couldn't be opened until the big day. It was put there intentionally by Michael Lindstrom and would be a useful psychological tool when it became time to negotiate wages and salaries. By building up their hopes and then causing the perception of delay in the hiring process, Michael knew that most would accept a lot less now than they would have over a year ago when the trailer had first been unveiled.

The new aluminum plant was magnificent—gleaming and state-of-the-art. It had that new car smell, a smell that was foreign to the residents. Many didn't own a car, and those who did, had to plead and cajole their well-aged vehicles to get them where they wanted them to go. That new car smell wouldn't last long when the smelting process began. Training would be starting in thirty days. Tours were arranged for the townspeople as well as the local and state government officials. Everyone agreed that this was a blessing and that the Lindstrom boys were a Godsend.

Michael had a flyer created and circulated to everyone that had been interviewed in the trailer. It called for a general meeting in the new mining company's auditorium. The gathering was to outline the wage and salary package that The Glacier Mining Company would be offering their new employees.

This meeting was the main subject in every home, pub, church and store. Everybody was speculating about what would happen and what would be offered. Hopes were high. To the workers in northwest Montana, a job was something temporary. Security was not the word that most people usually associated with employment in this part of the country. The Glacier Mining Company would hopefully break that cycle.

The day of the meeting had arrived, and the auditorium was jammed. Most had never been in a room that big before. It gave them a sense that the new company had the strength and staying power, usually lacking in the other companies in the valley.

Michael Lindstrom walked up to the podium and gave most of the potential workers their first look at one of the new owners. After introducing himself and his brother Brad and apologizing for John's absence, he began his prepared speech. John was already digging in the mine and was so excited about his progress that he had hardly spoken to Michael and Brad at all during the previous month. Besides, John was a geologist; what did he know about negotiating contracts and compensation packages for employees? Let the brothers do their thing; he would give them the biggest surprise that they could ever imagine. For once, John could have the undisputed bragging rights. His announcement would eclipse anything the three had ever done put together.

"Thank you all for coming out tonight," Michael began. "The Glacier Mining Company is excited to start mining ore from Teakettle Mountain and producing aluminum here in Hungry Horse. Most of you all have been interviewed by the company over the last three weeks, and we thank you for asking to join our family. Of course, not everybody will be hired, but I'm happy to say that most of you will. We will be talking with each of you tonight to let you know where you will fit in at the plant. All of you here tonight that took the time to interview will be asked to meet with one of our representatives this evening, whether or not you have been hired. Those of you who did not make the first cut have been put on a list to be called up in the event that we can't reach an agreement with those that did make the first cut. So don't leave early if you find that you have not been selected. We intend to reach an agreement with most of you tonight and to fill every available position. Whether or not you are hired will be your own business; we will not be posting anything for public view. As far as anyone will know, if you don't get a job, it is because you didn't like the compensation package."

The crowd liked what they'd heard so far, and no one expected any surprises. After all, the plant was almost finished, the investment was made, and certainly, the plant would be operating soon. The only uncertainty was what part of the process would they be involved with and what was to be their compensation. Most miners made $12.00 per day; certainly, they would make the same.

Michael continued, "I would like to share with all of you what our expectations are for this mine and plant. We're going to share with you the financial data and our projections so that you truly know the profits that we expect to make and how our success will affect your compensation."

The curtain rose behind the podium, and a series of charts and graphs were suddenly visible to the audience. The hand-painted charts and graphs were over eight feet tall and easily viewed. This theatrical production was all Brad.

Michael walked back to the podium after whispering something to his brother. "I would like to bring up my brother Brad to explain what all this means."

Brad was a handsome man, and at six feet four inches, he was an imposing figure. He exuded confidence and was the perfect choice to explain this new approach to paying employees.

The audience gave Brad warm applause, much warmer than the one that Michael received. Michael noticed. The brothers always carried a mental scorecard with them.

"I am delighted to share with you the sales and profit projections for The Glacier Mining Company. We intend for you to be the highest-paid mining and production workers in the world, and I am happy to show you how we are going to achieve that goal."

The excitement level in the building exploded. Brad was the best salesman these people had ever seen; they just didn't know it because they didn't realize that he was selling them something. It wasn't going to be a fair fight. When Brad was through with them, they would be eating out of his hand. The 'Brad Show' explained how profit sharing was the way that they all could make a lot of money. By sharing the profits that the charts and graphs projected, everybody would be happy. So what if their daily wage was below industry standards? The year-end bonus would equal the annual wage. The way Brad explained it, they would have to be crazy not to go along with it; after all, they would share in half of the net profits of the company. The fancy charts and graphs confirmed everything that Brad was telling them.

"At this time, I would like to hand out the employment agreements to everyone here." Brad smiled that smile that everybody loved and continued with his pitch. "Please read them carefully and take your time. If you have any questions, please come up to the podium so that someone may help you. We would like all of you to sign them if you are in agreement, even if you did not make the first cut. Remember, if our first choices don't sign up tonight, we will go to the next ones on the list. As I stated, it is our intention to fill every position this evening. I will not be going home tonight until every single position is filled."

This part was Brad's idea. A good salesman never leaves without a signature on the bottom line, and a great salesman knows that if you give someone time to think things over, you have given up control and will delay the outcome until a time pressure is established.

It worked like a charm. Almost all of the first choices signed up immediately because they knew that a signed contract would be waiting right behind them from the second choices. Brad had them right where he wanted them. They were gladly signing a below-market contract with promises of future wealth that would be totally controlled by Michael, because the profit sharing was based upon the net profits of the mine and plant. Brad didn't understand the power that his brother wielded over the employees. The net profits could be manipulated to show whatever they want them to be. The main objective of most accountants is to reduce net income or 'paper' profit so that low or no taxes will be due. Instead of doing it to avoid paying the IRS, they would now be doing it to avoid paying too much to their employees.

Brad figured that he was ahead on points as far as the Lindstrom brother's lifelong competition was concerned. It may have been Michael's plan and his idea to implement it, but it was Brad who sold it. Michael concealed his true motivation from Brad and was glad that it had been undetected.

The two of them executed over 679 labor contracts that night and returned originals to each applicant who accepted the offer. The two Lindstrom boys couldn't wait to tell their older brother the results.

As they left for the car, another explosion was heard coming from Teakettle Mountain. Michael and Brad looked at each other and smiled. They knew that John was still working in the mine, and they would have to wait to give him the good news. Michael usually bragged about his conquests, and this profit-sharing plan was one of his best ones yet.

The Vein

John couldn't believe what he was looking at. After the dust settled from the last blast, he couldn't catch his breath, not because of the blast, but because of what he was looking at. It was the largest vein of almost pure gold that he had ever seen or even heard about, and it seemed to go on forever. The last charge of the dynamite exposed what he had suspected was there from the beginning. He walked back to the entrance of the small test mine and tossed two sticks of lit dynamite back in. The mine entrance would be sealed for now, and he was the only one who knew about the gold.

John went home with the biggest grin his face could hold. The aluminum mine was all but forgotten now. The gold would be mined, and after they had extracted all of it from the mountain, they could begin the aluminum project. It might have to be postponed for ten years—there was that much gold. The three brothers had just become the richest men in the entire state of Montana!

No sooner had John walked in the door than the phone rang. It was Michael, and he couldn't wait till morning to tell John about the latest notch that he had carved into his gun belt. When Michael had finished telling John about the compensation package that included a profit-sharing plan, there was a mysteriously dead silence. "Hello? John, are you there?"

John had dropped the phone on the floor and was fumbling to pick it up again. His brothers had just made 697 employees extremely rich, along with the Lindstrom boys.

Hungry Horse, Montana, just became the wealthiest city per capita in the world.

John screamed into the phone, "You idiots, why didn't you tell me you would be offering a profit-sharing plan? I discovered a gold vein the size of a battleship tonight, and you just shared half of it with employees that haven't even shown up for their first day of work yet. We need to talk about this tonight! Nobody knows about the gold but me."

Michael was too shocked to respond to his brother's insult. He was experiencing the oddest emotion that he could imagine. It was as if he'd just won the lottery and suddenly remembered that he had promised to share his winnings with all his golf buddies. Sure, the generous proclamation sounded great at the time, but who would have thought he would actually win? Greed was a bad thing, and at least two of the Lindstrom boys had a bad case of it; only this time would their greed backfire.

"You're right, John," Michael said meekly. "We need to 'fix' this situation. Brad and I'll be right over."

"One other thing, Michael, bring a copy of the agreement."

John figured it would be a fairly simple task to conceal the gold. No one knew about it. Had John waited until the next day before setting off those last charges of dynamite, things would have been different. Too many people would have seen the gold vein, and it would have been impossible to hide. This was perfect; John and his brothers were the only ones who knew.

Michael knocked on the door with such force that John thought the neighbors would hear. "Hold on, I'm coming. The door's not locked," said John. Nobody locked their doors in Montana.

Michael pushed the door open and entered the house. The three brothers were expecting a heated discussion, and it looked like Michael would be leading the charge.

"Why on earth wouldn't you tell us about the gold vein? How dare you blame us for this fiasco." Michael was on the offensive, and John let him vent. "We busted our butts to get the employees we need for the aluminum production signed up at below-market wages, and you have withheld information that we could have used to structure things differently or even postpone the hiring process until we had a better handle on things! The most important part of our partnership has always been our openness and knowing what the others were up to."

"Are you finished?" John asked with that older brother's condescension that neither Brad nor Michael could stand.

"No, I'm not, John," Michael shot back. "You go off on your geological expeditions for over a month and keep everything a big secret. I know you and I know that you must have suspected you'd find gold in that mountain. You knew, and you didn't tell us."

"*Now* are you finished?" John repeated in a slightly less demeaning tone.

"Yeah, I'm finished for now." Michael left the door open for more salvos if he felt like it.

"What about the agreement, Mike?" John asked, wanting to defuse the situation. "What exactly does it say? There has got to be a way to get around this. We aren't operating a production facility to support a gold mine. It's for aluminum."

Michael didn't have any good news or suggestions for John. The agreement was airtight, and he knew it. "I'm not hopeful that we can get around the agreement. It plainly states that all net profits from all mining operations shall be shared and distributed on an equal basis between The Glacier Mining Company and its employees. If we were to fire all the employees today, we would have to equally share the net profits of all the gold."

"Guys, we screwed up!" Said Brad. "Let's just face up to our obligation and get on with business. We're rich, and so are our employees. I can think of a lot worse situations to be in."

"They don't deserve it!" Yelled John. "I found it, and it's ours alone. I won't give it to them. No one knows about it. I sealed the mine, and I'm gonna keep it sealed until we figure this thing out."

"I'm on your side, John," Michael said. "Let's figure this thing out before we make any decisions that we can't undo. Let's take our time and let things cool down between us. We didn't get where we are by making any rash decisions. From now on, we have got to be communicating more often. Our strength as a group lies in our individual talents. If we separate them, we will lose. What was it that Mom said when we started our first venture? One plus one plus one equals four. That's what she said, and she was right."

They all agreed to sleep on it for the time being. Brad was the only one who exhibited any disagreement. Michael and John took notice but didn't think that Brad's mind couldn't be changed.

Sleep

John and Michael tossed and turned all night long. Brad slept like a baby. In Brad's world, things were pretty simple, actually. The company had entered into an agreement, and that was that. As a salesman, he felt that his job was never finished. After the sale, he felt that it was his personal responsibility to make sure that the customer got what he bargained for. This situation was no different from any other sale he had made. Caveat Emptor was not a part of his business vocabulary. 'Let the buyer beware' was for a different class of salesmen.

Sure, the Lindstroms had tried to get the best deal they could, even if it would take a little money away from The Glacier Mining Company's new employees. Now, just because things took an unexpected and expensive twist didn't mean that they should try to get out of the deal. *We made a mistake, and I feel that we should live up to our agreement, Brad would say over and over again to himself.*

Brad was the only brother who seemed to clearly know right from wrong. Even at a very early age, Brad was never comfortable skirting the rules or cutting corners. He wasn't the type to give away an advantage, but he would never take excessive or unfair gain.

He wasn't at ease negotiating the profit-sharing plan that seemed to be weighted heavily to one side, but that didn't stop him from doing it. As a young man, he didn't have the maturity to combine all aspects of his life into the categories of right vs. wrong. He thought that business dealings had a different classification from his personal life. He got that idea from his older brothers, who were quite adept at dividing the playing field into manageable little enterprise zones.

Brad was coming into his own now and he would be listening more to his conscience instead of the rhetoric and slight-of-hand that seemed to be acceptable in business. Brad would strike many deals in the future that contained only an ethical promise, a firm handshake and a sincere look in the eyes. Brad didn't know how he would do it, but he would keep the game fair at the Glacier Mining Company. Or at least .. would do his best.

The Cover-up

Greed. This is what it all came down to for Michael and John. "I don't agree with you," Brad said the next day. Though he'd had a day to think about it, he still hadn't changed his mind.

"I can't fight it if you both overrule my vote." They set up their partnership with three equal votes to avoid stalemates and fights. "I think that it's wrong, and I'll live with your decision." Brad would live to regret this day.

The plan was simple to John. "I can purchase the 640 acres behind Teakettle Mountain for close to nothing. Remember the option contract we paid for before we formed the new mining company? The contract is in our name and not in the name of the Glacier Mining Company." Michael knew exactly what he had in mind and was already thinking about how he would structure the deal. "You're a genius!" Michael shouted. "We'll start a new mining company—a gold mining company—and go in and get the gold from the back of the mountain. We can process outside gold to make it look like all of the gold is brought in from outside the area."

"We will slowly work our way through Teakettle Mountain to reach the gold," John said with a smile on his face. "It's less than 1500 feet to the gold from the optioned land. It may take a few years longer than we would like, but if we work it right, no one will ever know."

Brad tossed in the last thread of conscience left out into the open. "It doesn't matter what door you go through when you rob the house. It's still stealing, and when you steal, there is always a chance that you will get caught."

"We won't get caught Brad," John replied. "I'll make sure of that. I can twist and turn the shaft so that no one will know what direction they're going once they are in the mine. I'll handle the entire operation."

"What if someone enters the shaft with a compass?" Asked Brad.

"I can magnetize the rail tracks so that no compass can function in the mine." John shot back his answer with such confidence that it seemed as if he could field any objection thrown his way. Brad was being outsold by his brother, the geologist.

Brad wasn't so sure that they wouldn't get caught and kept thinking of new objections to inject some sanity into this meeting. "How can we sell the gold if no one is supposed to know about it?"

This question was for Michael to handle, and he jumped on it with the same skill in salesmanship that John had just shown. "I can structure a brokerage deal and run the sale of gold through a third shell corporation to shield us."

Brad was losing at what he thought would be his last attempt at stopping this deceit. John had a different idea.

"Why don't we just leave it underground? We could refine it, pour it into ingots, and put them back into the mine shaft on our property. When the time is right, we'll move it and sell it."

"Why don't we try and cut a deal with the new workers?" Brad continued. "We could offer them an addendum to their agreement that would allow them to forgo the profit sharing and give them an increase in their salary. I would bet that almost every one of the workers would take the 'bird in the hand' scenario and opt out of the original deal—especially if we exceed industry pay standards."

"It won't work, Brad. If we were to go with your plan and someone found out that we knew about the gold, they could sue us to get back their original deal."

"I disagree," said Brad. "I think that even in that scenario, the judge would consider the fact that the employees had never worked a day and that it was an absolute windfall for them. We would still have the lion's share." Brad kept going. "How much money do we need, anyway? How much better can we live with $50 million instead of just $25 million?"

John and Michael looked at each other and just smiled. They thought that when Brad learned how much gold there was, he would be won over. Michael ran with it.

"Brad," Michael said. "There is over $1 billion worth of gold in the mine, as best John can tell, and you know John is never wrong. There may be more. We won't know until we dig."

"He might never be wrong about gold, but I think you're both wrong about concealing it," countered Brad. The amount of gold that was in the mine didn't change Brad's mind one bit.

"Brad, we won't get caught. We are the only ones who know about the gold, and we're family," John continued. "I can keep the gold locked up in the mine for fifty years if I want to, and no one will ever know. We can play out the aluminum mine in less than ten years if we decide and then close it down. We wait a few more years and then 'discover' the gold. Until then, we can still pull out millions through the shell corporation if we want to. It's a perfect plan."

Brad knew he would get nowhere with his brothers. The only other people more stubborn than Brad were his two siblings, and he was outnumbered and outvoted. If Brad were a religious man, he never said so. He couldn't hide the streak of conscience that he had inside of him. Brad always wanted to do what was right … and usually did. Even with hundreds of millions of dollars at stake, Brad was still stuck by his convictions. He wanted to do what was right.

None of the Lindstrom boys were married. Not that they weren't considered a prime catch. Just about every available female in Butte knew about the handsome, successful trio. Brad always stood out just a little more than John and Michael. His brothers thought it was his two-inch height advantage, but it wasn't. Something about Brad's character just seemed to shine through. He was always fair in grade school and didn't use his God-given gifts to take advantage of others. It carried through high school, college and was now starting to take hold in the world of business.

This was the first time that Brad considered doing something that he thought was so unfair and he knew that he would have a hard time putting it behind him and trying to forget about it. It wasn't the fear of getting caught that bothered him—it was the thought of harming someone that was tearing at his heart. For the first time, it seemed to Brad that he had just lost his two best friends. He felt an emptiness in his life. Brad knew that he should have no part in this arrangement and that the only right thing to do was to walk out on the deal.

If his brothers were worried about Brad, however, it certainly didn't show. In their minds, the money would bring happiness to them all. It was a simple equation, and as soon as the money started flowing, Brad would be glad that they outvoted him.

He wasn't, and Brad paid a price for not listening to his heart—a price that Michael and John wouldn't understand, a price that they would all eventually have to pay.

The Triangle 1985

Hungry Horse never struck it rich with the aluminum plant. The plant was not as successful as everyone had hoped. Just about 700 people worked there, and when it was averaged over the last thirty years, no one at the plant made more than the national average for mine workers. The profit-sharing plan worked just like Michael had expected. Since they controlled the expenses, they controlled the profits. John and Michael paid themselves enormous salaries even though the plant was run by others. Brad made a lot of money from the commissions that he earned for selling the finished metals. A company plane and other perks helped hold down the profits shared with the employees.

If it weren't for Brad's goading, the profits would have been even lower. Brad did everything in his power to keep the wages close to a fair market rate.

The valley grew up around them, and Hungry Horse was a stepchild to the other two towns, which didn't rely on one employer to put food on their tables. These three towns formed an unequal triangle.

A snow skiing resort opened on Lion Mountain, and the village of Whitefish Lake changed from a sleepy railroad town into a sleepy ski-and-tourist town. Whitefish Lake was only fourteen miles from Hungry Horse, but it might as well have been a world away. It wasn't exactly Aspen, but it was definitely chic by Montana standards anyway. Restaurants were upscale, and four golf courses and most of the shops catered to the summer crowd.

The people of Hungry Horse felt inferior to the small ski town, and they were constantly reminded that they were not in the same league.

Sixteen miles south on Highway 2 was the city of Kalispell, which started as a railroad town at the turn of the century. A population of over 20,000 people made it the largest city in a county that boasted a total population of 39,000. In Montana, it doesn't take much to boast. Kalispell was the county seat and had a varied employment base. Everything from technology companies to medical manufacturing and others in between resulted in a relatively stable work environment.

Hungry Horse had a deteriorating downtown and an aluminum plant that had lost its shine when the first meager profit-sharing checks were passed out in 1955. It had a chip on its shoulder and resented the way it was treated by the other two cities in the valley. It was a strange town. Half of the people were fairly well off. The other half made a meager living working in the plant.

The sign that proudly stated that Hungry Horse was the "Best Dam Town" was barely legible. It had never been repainted, and thirty years of weathering said it all. Hungry Horse was tired and worn out. Even the aluminum plant had lost its shine. Thirty years of smokestack pollution from the smelting process had killed off most of the vegetation from Teakettle Mountain. Hunters had known about the seriousness of the pollution for years and didn't bother hunting the elk and deer that lived near the plant. Almost every elk was terribly disfigured. Mostly, it was the ghastly-looking crooked teeth growing out of the side of their jaws that made it hard for the elk to eat properly, and as such, they had very little meat on their bones.

The gold processing plant on the backside of Teakettle Mountain was a small operation and was barely noticed by the town. With just twelve employees, it wasn't much, even though it was the fifth-largest non-government employer in town. John spent most of his time in the mine and had accumulated over 625,000 pounds of gold during the last thirty years. John kept the turnover high and his usual group of three mine workers never worked for more than six months at a time before he would find a reason to send them packing. He never hired anyone from the local labor force. He always paid them double wages, and no one was ever led to believe that their job would last for more than six months. As far as anyone knew, the gold was trucked in and processed.

John would refine the gold himself after the small group of workers left and poured it into bullion bricks, storing them in a hidden shaft in the mine. He had over 12,500 ingots there. Gold was his life, and he was never happier than when he could be close to his gold. John never married, and now, at sixty-two, no one expected that he would. Besides, he was getting stranger and stranger every year. It was his gold doing it.

The gold was running out, and John felt that it would soon be over. He had put up less than fifty ingots in 1984, and this year, he would be lucky to add ten ingots to the stash. He was the only one actually working in the mine now, and his secretary and bookkeeper were the only ones left working in the office. Bobby, the security guard, was the last one on the grounds.

It was time to cash in on thirty years of clandestine work. John was so proud of himself that no one knew what was really going on in the gold production facility except for Michael. Even Brad didn't know a thing about it. Every time they tried to broach the subject with him, he wouldn't have anything to do with it. He told them that it was wrong and that the gold should be shared with the aluminum plant workers.

Brad wanted no part of their scheme and no part of the gold. He had said it from the beginning and he hadn't changed his mind. Nothing could be better as far as John and Michael were concerned. More for them.

The Sale

The gold was running out, and the aluminum plant actually had a good year. It was time to sell. Brad was the youngest at fifty-four, and John and Michael were in their early sixties. Selling the aluminum plant would make it a lot easier to take the gold out undetected. Brad liked the idea of selling the company because the employees would share in the gain. It was valued at over $140 million, which meant that, on average, each employee would receive a check for $100,000. Most of the employees had been there from the beginning, and the replacement workers would share with the earlier employees on a pro-rata basis. Some families had five or six workers at the plant and would reap a bonanza.

In a short time, four bidders surfaced with an interest in buying the plant. Michael was eager to work on structuring the deal. The Lindstrom boys would each stand to receive over $23 million. The value of the gold was over $4 billion. The Lindstroms were very wealthy by all accounts before the sale. The profit from the aluminum plant just added a little more to their ledgers. The gold would be an impressive addition. An addition that nobody would know about.

A deal was struck with an out-of-state company. The sale price would net over $146 million. $73 million was to be equally split with 702 employees. The average check would be just under $104,000.

The attorneys were called in to reduce the structured deal to writing. It was estimated that the entire process would take about six months to close. Checks would be distributed at that time. Hungry Horse and the 'triangle,' along with the entire valley, would soon be going through some changes.

Kathleen

Brad had been married for twenty-six years to a wonderful woman whom he met at the aluminum plant. Kathleen was the most beautiful person that he had ever seen. She worked in the summer as a temp during high school and as a nurse when she graduated from college. She had saved more than one life in her ten years on the job at the plant. She was one of the few Hungry Horse residents to go to college and actually return to live and work in the community.

Brad had 'lost' two brothers to their greed thirty years earlier, but gained a soul mate when he met and married Kathleen. He first saw her when she was just seventeen during her summer work at the plant. He noticed that she wasn't working that next summer, and he actually missed her. This was a first for Brad.

Kathleen ended up taking a summer job with a wealthy industrialist and his wife in New York. She got the job through Dante, a college friend that worked in the summer for the Phillips and was always on the lookout for other summer employees. Mrs. Phillips kept a staff of eighteen in her summer home and Kathleen would be an upstairs maid working in the west wing.

The trip to New York was the first time Kathleen had ever left the western states. Flying into La Guardia Airport after circling Manhattan was an unbelievable experience. The Empire State Building, the Statue of Liberty and the Brooklyn Bridge were impressive. Most people from small towns are intimidated by Manhattan. Kathleen wasn't.

The Phillips sent her the airline tickets to New York. If Kathleen had had her way, she would take a train home. The DC 3 went through two electrical storms in the Midwest, and that scared her more than the grizzly bears she occasionally encountered in the mountains near her home. The first storm was during daylight, and she went through it reasonably unscathed. The second one was after dusk, and the sight of the lightning that nearly touched the wings and turbulence that shook the plane was truly terrifying to her.

The Phillips' limousine was waiting to pick her up at baggage claim. Dante was the driver, and she was glad to see him again. They drove up to Connecticut to catch the ferry boat from New London that would take them out to Fisher Island.

The twenty-minute ferry ride ended at a simple dock on the west side of the island. The limousine slowly pulled out of the lower level of the ferry and lumbered up to the disembarking area. The ride up to the house was like nothing that she could have dreamed. Huge mansions, or summer 'cottages' as they were called, were everywhere. You could only catch little glimpses through the gates, and some were so secluded that there was no hint of their majesty from the street.

The Phillips house was known as the 'Summer Wind' and was well-known on the island. A letter could be simply addressed to:

Summer Wind

Fisher Island, New York

Delivery would be a certainty.

Mr. Phillips had made a fortune in the battery industry. He was 84 years old when he sold the company in 1975. It had over 30,000 employees worldwide. The 'Summer Wind' attested to the Phillips' power and wealth, and this was just a summer home for three months out of the year. With over forty rooms, it was magnificent. Kathleen would be responsible for three of those rooms.

Working for the Phillips family was like going to finishing school. Kathleen soon discovered that she knew very little about the wealthy and the various rituals that set them apart from just about everyone else.

She learned more in that summer than she could have learned in a lifetime in Montana.

Kathleen started work for the Phillips family in early June of 1955 and was expected to stay on until Labor Day. Her pay was $20 per week and she soon became the favorite of Mr. and Mrs. Phillips. Mrs. Phillips was considerably younger than Mr. Phillips and his advancing years made her very careful with his situation. His frailty made her very nervous, and because of that, she would always bring Kathleen with her whenever they went out. It was on one of those outings that a terrible accident happened. Mr. Phillips always acted like he was a lot younger than his years. You could say he still had a spark in him. They were returning home when the Checker Marathon limousine pulled up to the front entrance of the mansion, and Mr. Phillips jumped out of the back seat almost like he was showing off. He stumbled immediately and fell down, breaking his hip.

The rest of the summer was a sad time for Kathleen. She watched helplessly as Mr. Phillips' health and spirits faded away. Mrs Phillips was so upset, causing her to be very difficult to work with. One by one, the staff broke their agreements and deserted her. Kathleen probably would have done the same had she not needed the money for nursing school. She stayed and was glad she did. The Phillips needed her, and if she had any doubts about her calling to be a nurse, they had vanished. Taking care of Mr. Phillips made her feel happy and much more useful than taking care of three upstairs bedrooms. She was soon the only employee left. Her job description changed from upstairs maid to nurse, cook, driver, head housekeeper and confidant. Mrs. Phillips convinced her to skip her first semester of nursing school classes and stay on to help. Kathleen was anxious to start school, but she couldn't leave them with a clear conscience.

She stayed on through Thanksgiving and then said her goodbyes—goodbye to Mrs. Phillips for the first time and goodbye to Mr. Phillips for the last time. Kathleen knew that she would never see him again and worried for Mrs. Phillips. She hoped that she would be invited back the next summer to work for her again, but when she left and collected her pay, she saw that the customary bonus had not been included. Kathleen felt as if her help and commitment to the Phillips weren't appreciated. After all, she had done the work of the entire staff without a raise and even stayed on at the expense of missing her first term at school. She knew Mrs. Phillips to be tough but fair, and now Kathleen felt that she might have made a mistake in not starting school in September.

Kathleen arrived home in Hungry Horse during the first week of December. The train trip took three long, tiresome days. A message was waiting from Mrs. Phillips, who confirmed what she knew was coming. Mr. Phillips had quietly passed away in his sleep.

There was no snow on the ground, and everything looked dark and bleak except for the tops of the snow-covered peaks that surrounded the dam and reservoir. Clouds would be ever-present until the spring. She would try to resume school in the winter term. Enough money had been saved to pay for two terms with room and board.

After sitting around the house for two days, she went out to visit friends in town and stopped by the plant during the lunch whistle. Brad noticed Kathleen right away and walked over to her. She thought that she was in trouble for being in the plant lunchroom. The sign over the door read 'Employees Only', and she wasn't one anymore. Instead, Brad welcomed her back and asked if she was home from school. She wasn't proud that she missed her first term, but under the circumstances, she wasn't ashamed. Brad offered her a job right away if she wanted one, and she seemed interested. It was left that she would contact him after the first of the year. Kathleen was intrigued by Brad and was teased by her girlfriends in the lunchroom. He always seemed so unobtainable and besides, no one had ever seen him out socially with a woman. She thought nothing more about it.

Maybe she would stay and work for the next year. It was time to leave the lunchroom, and the third whistle confirmed that. Her friends made plans to visit her over the weekend. Kathleen slowly made her way back home.

Kathleen was surprised when she walked up the stairs to her home. The big black Cadillac out on the curb was certainly a novelty in Hungry Horse, unlike Fisher Island. Here, they were not your standard mode of transportation. Kathleen's mother, Bridget, met her at the door and hurried her in. There, she met Mr. Crenshaw. He explained that his law firm had been retained by Mrs. Phillips to help facilitate her educational plans. Kathleen sat stunned as he explained that her entire education had been paid for by Mrs.Phillips, as well as her room and board. He went on to explain that her books, clothing, and even spending money had been included in the budget. Not stopping there, he also informed her that she had been accepted at the Henry Ford Hospital School of Nursing in Detroit, Michigan and that they would be expecting her on January 4, 1956. Special arrangements had been made to make up her first term and to launch her into the second term fully prepared by the first two weeks in February. Mr. Crenshaw handed Kathleen a stack of books that would prepare her for her task. Included in the package was a booklet of train tickets that included a round-trip ticket to New

London, Connecticut, in June with a return ticket for the end of August. It looked like she got her job back after all.

Mr. Crenshaw explained that he had something else in the car for her and excused himself. Kathleen sat staring at her mother in complete shock. Mr. Crenshaw returned with a huge train trunk. How he got that out of the back of his Cadillac was a riddle. He brought it in and opened it up, revealing a complete wardrobe for her school year, including six nursing uniforms, four cocktail dresses and two evening gowns. The only thing missing was a diamond tiara.

Mr. Crenshaw explained everything and had Kathleen sign a receipt of acceptance. He had a great story to tell at the office when he returned to Helena the next day, and Kathleen had a great story to tell her family and friends in Hungry Horse.

Kathleen asked her mom if she could make a long-distance call to thank Mrs. Phillips. Normally that would have been out of the question. Long distance was very expensive and a letter would do just fine. This, of course, was something out of the ordinary and so Kathleen called Irma down at the switchboard to start the ball rolling. Kathleen had the numbers that Mrs. Phillips had given her when she left Fisher Island. One was for her Park Avenue apartment in Manhattan, and the other was for her winter home in Eleuthera Island, Bahamas. She decided to try the New York number first, and after about ten minutes, Irma had a connection. The maid answered the phone, and soon she heard the voice of her fairy godmother. She also could tell that Irma was still on the line and thanked her for her help. Irma didn't say anything and quickly hung up, but the tell-tale click gave her away.

Kathleen thanked her for everything she had done for her. Mrs. Phillips quickly cut the gushing short and thanked Kathleen for sticking by her in her time of need. Kathleen asked about Mr. Phillips and learned that he had quietly passed away the day she had left Fisher Island. Kathleen expressed her sadness and, after regaining her composure, said that she was hoping to help him next summer when she would be returning to work at the house.

Mrs. Phillips asked her what on earth she meant, and Kathleen felt foolish. She assumed that the ticket was for her to return to her job, and now she was embarrassed.

"You'll do no such thing, my dear!" Her forceful tone and manner being conveyed over 3,000 miles of cable made it clear that Kathleen wouldn't be working the next summer. "You will be staying with me at 'Summer Wind' as my guest for the season, and from now on, you will call me by my first name. Oh, and don't forget to bring the gowns and cocktail dresses—you'll need them."

"Thank you, Mrs. … I mean, Margaret." There was that missing tiara. Now Kathleen was a bona fide princess, and she was ready to accept the title along with all of the work and benefits that came with her new appointment.

Brad and Kathleen were married in 1959. Margaret Phillips attended the ceremony. Their relationship blossomed into something special. To Margaret, Kathleen was the daughter that she never had, but always wanted.

The Lawyers

Funny things start happening when you get lawyers involved. They start asking a lot of questions, and all of a sudden, those questions create even more questions.

It all started innocently when it was noticed that the sale of the Glacier Mining Company didn't include the Teakettle Mountain land. The title was to remain with the Lindstrom family. This seemed like a formality at first, but when the Lindstroms resisted including the land in the sale, people started wondering why.

Rumors of gold had been circulating for years. It always seemed strange that a gold processing plant would be located so far from the source of gold. Fueling the rumor was the mysterious gold processing operation that didn't employ any local production workers and had an incredibly high turnover rate for the few workers that they employed. When the brothers offered to pay market rates for the land to retain the title, suspicions grew even more intense. The Lindstroms never paid "retail" for anything, and if they wanted the Teakettle Mountain land, then something was in that land.

The purchasers of the aluminum plant had accepted the explanation that the mountain contained no usable ore; after all, that was the story for the last thirty years. They didn't care either way; with the railroad delivering ore from mines across the state at a cheap rate, it really wasn't important if it came from the land behind the plant or from another county. The attorneys for the purchasers did insert a clause into the purchase agreement that gave them a first right of refusal on any ore that might be mined in the future. This innocuous clause became a deal breaker with the Lindstroms, and the purchasers backed down. They had, after all, signed the deal and had over $30 million invested in their due diligence and earnest money. If they held their ground, they could risk forfeiting over $24 million in earnest money. This was a done deal, and a new clause wasn't going to stop it.

The attorneys for the workers must have sensed something, because they insisted on bringing in another law firm that specialized in employee buyouts. This out-of-town firm was especially adept at exposing carefully concealed assets and had great skill at valuing them. When the sale changed from a total sale to a sale that held back certain assets for the owners, they knew that they would need help, and to protect themselves as much as the employees, they insisted on bringing in the big guns.

A meeting was called with the past and present workers to decide if this new direction should be taken—a new direction that would slow down the sale and allow a more careful inspection of the books and assets of the aluminum plant. This was a risky business, and a lot of the workers had been spending money before they had it. Just looking out in the parking lot of the plant revealed over a hundred new pickup trucks and other assorted new vehicles. Quite a few of these faithful workers had amassed some formidable debt, courtesy of their local lenders, and if the deal was delayed, so would the payments on their new toys. Purchase agreements had been entered into for new homes and land, and now a lot of people were getting nervous about the potential problems that a delay would bring.

After three hours, a resolution was narrowly passed that authorized the new law firm to come in and assess the situation. Based on their findings, the deal would close quickly … or take more time— possibly a lot more time. Their compensation would come from a percentage of any additional assets that they could uncover and would not reduce the employees' original deal. The attorneys notified all parties of the new resolution, and the legal jousting began.

The representatives for the purchaser insisted that any delay would affect the value of the plant and reminded the employees' attorneys that they had signed a deal. The Lindstrom brothers' attorneys raised the same objection and threatened litigation if they attempted to thwart the deal.

The employees had no intention of calling off the deal; in fact, they wanted to proceed quickly. Their actions were not aimed at harming anyone. They would close on schedule; they simply wanted the revenue from the sale held by the courts until the Teakettle Mountain situation could be examined more carefully, along with the books of the gold mining operation. The new owners could proceed as intended without interference. If the attorneys for the employees were satisfied that everything was fair and honest, then the money would be released immediately to both parties. If they felt that it was not fair, then the courts would have to decide for them.

The mood of the Lindstroms had been shattered. They knew that the State of Montana had sided with the workers in almost every situation, no matter how ludicrous it was. The state was known for its conservative stand on just about everything else. It balanced it out by always taking a liberal stance with the workforce. It granted them anything they wanted on a regular basis. In this instance, the state would be justified.

Midas

John, Michael and Brad all knew that this day would come, but only Brad admitted it out loud to his brothers.

They had not told a soul about the gold, which was just fine for John and Michael, but Brad had always felt it was wrong not to share this with the employees, and it always bothered him that he had not told his wife. They shared everything and their married life together had been as happy as either one had ever dreamed of. Now, he wished that he had exhibited the courage to tell her long before. He knew that he would have to tell her now.

"The way I see it, we have two options," Michael blurted out. "We either move the ingots now and cover our tracks in the mine or take our chances with the courts."

"I say we move the gold out. We don't stand a chance in court," John said emphatically. "All they need is the judge to grant them access to the property, and we're sunk!"

They two brothers shot Brad a pathetic look. Brad looked fifteen years younger than his two older brothers. He didn't have the same lines and creases on his face. Brad still slept like a baby at night. He never thought about the gold, never made plans to spend it, never gave it any prominence in his life or in his plans for the future. He had more money than he could spend and as it was, he was giving most of it to his church and various charities.

"There is one more option, and it's flawless." Brad had them both sitting up straight, poised for the news. "Tell them about the gold. Just tell the truth." As Brad said it, he gave them a look that reminded them of their father when he was ashamed of something that his boys had done in grade school.

"I'm not just telling you this because I know that you're going to get caught. I'm telling you this because this is the only way that you will be able to actually have a chance of enjoying the gold," Brad said sincerely. He still loved his brothers; he just didn't like them so much anymore.

"Look at yourselves! This gold has almost ruined your lives. It's all you two think about. You don't love anything more than your gold!"

They all knew the story of Midas—it was one of John's favorites as a young boy. Hopefully this modern rendition of the story would not end so tragically.

John and Michael were more nervous now than ever. Brad would be trouble; he had too much character to be able to put this away into a small compartment and distance himself from it. John and Michael had character when it was needed for something they wanted or for those things that didn't require any courage.

The quiet was uneasy. Brad broke the awkward silence. "I won't be any part of this scheme. I don't want any of the gold, and under these circumstances, I couldn't accept it. We made a deal with the employees, and we should abide by it."

The two brothers knew Brad well enough to know that it might eventually come to this. He told them before that he wasn't interested in his share without including the others. "As far as I'm concerned, I was never a part of your side deal, and I don't consider myself a part of it now!"

"Do what's right." Brad knew he wasn't connecting with his brothers, which only made him angry. This was the hardest sale he had ever attempted, and he was failing miserably. He knew he would. Greed always killed a deal. It didn't matter if it was the buyer or seller; if greed got in the way, Brad knew that he would never be able to structure a fair deal. The deal with the employees was haunting him now, and it looked like everybody would end up a loser—but not if Brad had anything to say about it.

He would let his brothers talk it over together, get some sleep, and meet with them again in the morning. He would not give up. The stakes were too high. If his brothers kept on the same path, Brad knew they would get caught, which would certainly mean jail time.

The Truth

Kathleen knew that something was wrong. Brad wasn't himself. She was looking forward to the sale because she and Brad had planned to take a year off and travel together—just the two of them without the constant interruption of the mine and the brothers. Both Kathleen and Brad felt that they were being called to do something positive for people who needed help. This calling had been slowly building for the last ten years, and now it was getting much more intense. Brad was fifty-four years old now, and when he died, he didn't want to be remembered as that aluminum salesman who became rich.

Kathleen and Brad had become deeply religious over the years, and their beliefs had given them a new way to look at their lives and the lives of those around them. Brad wasn't an "in your face" type of religious man. He simply did what was right and became an example to others.

If someone swore in the office, he wouldn't chastise them. He didn't have to; Brad was persuasive and could be very subtle when achieving his goals. His reaction would typically be one that made the offender feel that he or she was a better person than that, and that swearing or telling off-color jokes was unbecoming to them. To Brad, there was no other way to handle these situations. He had been a real rebel in college and had done many things in his early years that he was not proud of. How could he take a "holier than thou" approach, knowing that he himself was no angel. Brad was a leader by example, not by words.

In 1980, Brad and Kathleen both had experiences that made them aware of deep changes in themselves were taking place.

Brad's experience happened at the Spokane, Washington, airport while waiting to board an airplane with three others from the aluminum plant. The plane arrived on time at the gate, but no one was getting off the plane. Suddenly, four county sheriffs came running down the terminal corridor and flew past the gate entrance onto the plane. Five minutes later, the sheriffs had a man in handcuffs. This young man was yelling, fighting, and screaming obscenities at the officers. The man was so drunk that he couldn't even stand on his own. It was only eleven in the morning. Shortly after that, a woman in tears left the plane. She had obviously known him and began to follow them.

Brad genuinely empathized with this person whom he had never met before. Normally Brad would have shown his disgust for what had happened and would likely have joined in the crowd's laughter and ridiculed the man along with his three travelling partners and all of the other people who had just witnessed the scene. But this time, it was different, and so was Brad.

His travel partners were laughing and tapping Brad on the shoulder to get his reaction to the fiasco. But Brad seemed to be almost in a trance. When they finally got Brad's attention, he seemed surprised—not that everyone was looking at him, but by the fact that he had been praying for this man, praying so hard that the world around him seemed to vanish.

Brad excused himself and followed the group out to the waiting squad cars. He picked up his prayer and reiterated it with much more intensity, continuing as the police drove away with the man.

He looked around and noticed that most everyone who had witnessed this drunken, disorderly man being placed into a squad car, had been laughing at him. He felt out of place in the airport—and in the world, too, for that matter.

He returned to the gate where his companions had been anxiously waiting for him. They weren't laughing anymore. They learned from a passenger who knew the young man what had happened and told Brad the whole story.

It turns out that he was indeed drunk and under the influence of four prescription sleeping pills. His name was Alan Snyder and he was from Boise, Idaho. He was on his way to a rehab center in California. Alan had been binge drinking for seven weeks to fight the guilt and depression he felt.

His fiancée had committed suicide seven weeks earlier after a terrible accident that left her younger sister in a coma with no hope for recovery—an accident that had been his fault.

When Brad learned the terrible story about this lost soul, it didn't make him feel any better that he hadn't laughed at him. It made him all the sadder, and he prayed for him on the hour-long flight back to the Kalispell airport. And he prayed that evening. And for months after that. Brad was never the same after that encounter.

Kathleen had had an equally intense experience during the same week. She had become close to God over the years but was still separated by a series of incidents. A good friend of hers had been spreading lies about her and Brad, and she felt betrayed. Her anger was like a wall, and she knew it. It distressed her, and it was affecting her sleep. This person had moved from the valley, and although she had burned many bridges before departing and lost credibility with most of the people that she knew, Kathleen couldn't let go of it. She was experiencing menacing dreams and was at a loss for a way out of her pattern of anger and hostility. While Brad was away on his business trip, Kathleen decided to use prayer as a shield and as a weapon to confront the evil head-on and tear down the wall that her heart had been constructing.

It worked. She found that when she prayed for her friend, she was able to turn her thoughts away from herself and direct them toward the one who needed to be blessed. In her prayers, she forgave her, and that brought an end to the destructive dreams, anger and hostility.

Kathleen would remember that episode as a turning point in her life, and the way that she would approach problems in the future was colored by that day. It was a milestone week for both of them and signaled the beginning of a new way of looking at and dealing with the world around them.

Kathleen and Brad were searching for something more, and they both felt that a breakthrough was close. Their two experiences five years ago were a "God thing," as they put it, and now, when they prayed, they listened for God as much as they spoke to Him.

That night, Brad told Kathleen about the gold and his brothers' scheme to conceal it. They both knew what had to be done.

The Breakup

The three Lindstrom boys met early in the morning at Michael's house. It was painfully obvious that no one had changed his mind on how to proceed.

After more than an hour of lobbying on both sides, the two brothers had enough of Brad's "nonsense." They accepted Brad's statement that he had never made a claim to any gold that wasn't split with the employees. Just to tidy things up a bit, the brothers drafted a letter simply stating that Brad was not claiming anything more than his rightful split from the sale of the aluminum plant and that all business ties between them would be severed after the sale and distribution of funds. It went on to indemnify each other and hold all parties harmless in the event that a dispute arose at a later date. At the brother's insistence, no mention of gold was in the letter. Two copies were made, and all three signed the letter. Michael's gardener witnessed all three signatures twice.

Brad said his goodbyes and left his two brothers alone. He still loved them very much, but things would never be the same with them. He felt that he was saying goodbye to them for good, and that made him very upset.

"Why couldn't they be satisfied with splitting $2 billion in gold instead of $4 billion." The whole thing was absurd. You couldn't possibly spend $2 billion in your lifetime, let alone $4 billion. A string of crimes would be necessary to achieve their goals, not to mention the fact that the IRS would surely be suspicious of anyone attempting to spend those kinds of sums.

Brad didn't think that they had been taking any gold out and selling it, but who knew? Maybe they had. He asked his brothers if they had sold any, and they both insisted that they had not. Brad was thankful that he wasn't a part of their scheme.

He checked in at the office, but it was a totally wasted day. No one at the plant seemed very eager to work. The place was filled with unfamiliar faces. Some long-time employees had quit and took an early retirement, knowing that they would soon be receiving a windfall. Their replacements were everywhere, and that added to the strangeness of it all. Everything was upside down at the plant, and almost everything in Brad's life was upside down, too. Thank God for Kathleen. Six months from now, they would start a new phase of their life together, and it was looking more enticing than ever.

Brad arrived home at 3:30 in the afternoon and was pleased that Kathleen was home. They had a lot to talk about. Brad had come to the conclusion that he would have to tip off the attorneys for the employees that there was gold in Teakettle Mountain.

"I can't let my brothers go to jail, Kathleen. They are so blinded by greed that they can't make a rational decision. They will be caught, and they will spend years in prison—maybe even die there." Brad gave Kathleen a look that she had never seen before. It was total fear.

Kathleen tried to ease his misery by rubbing his neck and shoulders. "I have never seen you so tense." Kathleen knew the answer to her question but asked it anyway. "So, what are you going to do about it?"

"I'm going to tip off the workers. It's the only way to keep my brothers out of jail and do what's fair at the same time." There it was. He said it, and he knew that betrayal was the only course of action. He was surprised that he had the courage to do it. Kathleen wasn't. When they were dating, she was attracted to Brad's character as much as his good looks. She hadn't made a mistake in marrying him.

They both decided an anonymous tip was better than a direct shot. Brad wanted to save his brothers and, at the same time, save their relationship. He would call the attorney first thing in the morning. "No," he thought to himself. "I'd better do it now. No telling what my brothers might be planning." John and Michael were much too resourceful, intelligent and impulsive to wait even an hour. Brad walked to his study and picked up the phone. There was no turning back now.

He phoned Henry Peyton, the attorney for the employees, and told him enough to interest him. Henry wasn't easily fooled by anyone, and this story had the markings of an obvious prank. Brad was prepared for this reception; especially from a seasoned pro like Henry.

"Station four men outside the gates of the gold mine and have them follow anyone that leaves. If they see a truck leave, don't let it out of their sight. Make sure your men have a CB radio so that they can call for help if they need to. You'll find John and Michael Lindstrom there. Make sure someone is there 24 hours a day until you get the judge to grant you an inspection. You'll find what you're looking for in the mine shaft. If I need to contact you again, I will use the name 'mother lode'."

"Tell me one more thing before you hang up," Peyton said with a much more respectful tone. "Why are you telling me this?"

"So I can look at myself in the mirror," Brad said, and he meant it. "And by the way, don't give a percentage of the find to the out-of-town lawyers. At the very least, cap the amount that they can earn at half a million. There's one more thing: don't repeat what we talked about to anyone, or you will never hear from me again."

Peyton heard the click signaling that the mysterious caller had hung up, and he did the same. He just sat there for a couple of minutes trying to figure it all out.

"Motherlode!" He screamed, and at once, he knew that the mine didn't just process ore like everybody was led to believe. Teakettle Mountain had ore in it all right, but it wasn't just aluminum. It was gold, and there must have been a lot of it.

Brad had done it. Hopefully, it would save his brothers from spending time at Deer Lodge State Penitentiary. He thought that was such a pleasant name for a prison. It sounded like a hunting lodge. In a way, it was. Criminals were hunted down and given free lodging for years at a time.

Peyton jumped into action and found four men to immediately drive to the mine and post guard. The next call was the judge. He was putting his reputation on the line, and he knew it. He believed the story that the "mother lode" had spun. Now, he had to convince the judge of the same story. How could he do it without telling the judge about this mysterious "mother lode"? He would find a way.

Judge Costa was one of the few female judges in Montana. Henry had been one of her biggest supporters when she was appointed to the bench, and she never forgot it. Henry had never taken advantage of his help. Today though, he might have to "redeem a coupon" to get the judge to go along with this one.

The next call was to the outside counsel. He put their deal on hold until things settled down a bit.

Gold Fever

Judge Costa went along with Henry Peyton's request. They both knew that his "coupon" had now been fully redeemed. Henry, and the judge for that matter, hoped that it was worth it. A relatively large chunk of their professional reputation depended on it.

The guards at the mine entrance stopped the two brothers in their tracks. They were smart enough to stay away for the time being. When John tried to scare them off, Henry knew that he was on to something big and that made him feel some relief.

The brother confronted Brad with the news and asked him outright if he had tipped off the attorneys. "I have done nothing wrong, and I don't want to hear another word about the gold. I am not a part of your scheme and I don't want to be dragged into it." Brad said this with a clear conscience. He didn't want to lie to them and he didn't. "Your plan is unraveling, and you had better think about the future. They must be on to you, and if they aren't yet, they will be."

In a strange way, Michael was relieved that the whole thing would be ending soon. Michael regained the use of his right brain again and he was smart enough to understand the downside of their scheme now that people were camping at the mine entrance and following them. John was a different matter. His success as a geologist was a combination of education and instinct. He was still convinced that they would prevail in court and have their gold. Michael was smart enough to know that it was a lot easier to hide the gold than it was to get it out and spend it; especially if people were suspicious. The IRS would audit them forever, and if it was found out that they purchased more than they declared in their tax returns, you could be sure that a criminal investigation would be close behind.

Michael got cold feet and it was the best thing that had ever happened to him. He would have a lot of explaining to do, but that was better than looking over his shoulder for the rest of his life.

"I'm going back to the mine," John announced. Michael and Brad weren't ever surprised by anything that John said or did.

"I want you to do something for me," Michael asked him to fire up the old forklift, divide the ingots into two equal stacks and to stand back and look at the gold again. "After you do that, divide one of the stacks in half again. If you don't think that a $1 billion stack of gold is enough for you to live on happily, then you come back and tell me." Michael had him. How could he argue that it wasn't? Brad thought that Michael was brilliant. Let him see exactly how much his share would be. Words just didn't compare to the visual impression. Michael was a pretty good salesman, after all.

Brad and Michael didn't actually think that John would divide the gold into stacks, but that's exactly what he did. He went past the "guards" posted at the gates of the mine and headed straight into the mine and spent the rest of the day and a good part of the night finishing the task.

When he stood back and saw the size of his stack, he changed his mind. It was more than any human could spend in a lifetime. It was enough gold for one man. He knew that he would never spend it anyway. He just wanted to look at it. If they had been steel bars painted gold, he probably would have been just as happy. Just like Midas, he wished he could return to the past and rethink what he had done. He was glad that it was over too, and just like Michael, he felt the weight of the gold being lifted off his shoulders. The gold fever had broken, and he felt better about himself than he had in thirty years.

Even though it was the fear of getting caught that changed their minds, Brad was still humbled by their change of heart. He had his brothers' backs, and that was worth more than gold.

The three met the next morning and started to sort it out. There had to be a way for them to save a little dignity.

Brad didn't care; he just wanted to call up the attorneys and tell them everything. John and Michael wanted to find a way to save face. Brad would let them wrestle with that one on their own. He did make it clear that he would not be a part of any lies. "After all, it's not my gold, and I never had a claim to it."

Brad suggested that they spend the day in the office, and he would help them package their story. This was really going to be an interesting sales pitch. Brad wanted this whole mess sewn up that evening so that an announcement could be made the next day.

The Explanation

The two brothers hadn't come up with any explanation that didn't have a lie or two weaved throughout. How could you paint a nice picture on a canvas that had been covered with dirt and left in a mine shaft for thirty years? There wasn't much to work with.

This confession would take more courage and character than John and Michael could muster. Brad insisted on the truth, and no other explanation would suffice.

"I'll stand up and handle this for you," Brad said without much enthusiasm.

"You have a plan?" Michael asked. He was sure that it would be a pretty painful and embarrassing, but maybe Brad would spare them a total humiliation with a little fib or two.

"I don't have a 'plan,' Michael. I'm going to tell the truth. I told you before that I will not lie. Lying will backfire. Look what happened to Nixon. If he hadn't lied and tried to cover up the Watergate break-in committed by others, he would have served out his term with dignity. I'm not going to let that happen here."

"Please Brad, this isn't the presidency we're talking about. There has to be a way to get us off the hook." Michael was not ready for the public spectacle that Brad seemed to be arranging for them.

"Let's hear your plan before we continue to speculate." John didn't even look up when he spoke to Brad. He sensed that his younger brother wouldn't send them out to be slaughtered. John didn't really seem to care what anyone thought. He could easily slink out of town and move to someplace with a warm climate and never look back. I think that it would be best if you were there."

John showed no emotion, while Michael flinched at the thought of a public flogging.

"I'll explain that two of us wanted to hide the gold, and one of us didn't. I'll start at the beginning. The whole story about signing up the employees and then coming home to discover that John had found a modern-day mother lode; how it didn't seem fair that the Lindstroms had risked their own capital to bring jobs to Northwest Montana and that the profit-sharing plan would take away a huge windfall that wasn't even a part of the aluminum production. I think that they will understand. I won't disclose who was for hiding the gold and who was against it. We will all be tarnished, but we won't be despised.

"You mean to say that you won't tell anyone that you were the one to go against the plan?" Michael was astounded at his younger brother's offer to share in their misery and share the blame in a way that made it manageable and bearable.

"I give you my word." They knew that they could trust Brad.

"Let's get this behind us as soon as possible before Judge Costa grants the employees the right to inspect the gold mine." Brad wanted to leave no way for the brothers to change their minds and start backtracking. "I'm going home to collect my thoughts and start the ball rolling. I don't want to change my mind on this, and if I start it tonight, I won't be able to." Brad knew he would never change his mind, but it wouldn't hurt to let his brothers think that he might get cold feet. It would make them want to do it his way, now more than ever.

The three shook hands on the deal and looked each other in the eye again for the first time in years.

Kathleen was waiting anxiously when Brad arrived home. When she saw a smile on Brad's face, she knew that they had worked out a way to put an end to the deceit.

"Tell me everything. What have the Lindstroms decided to do?" Kathleen couldn't contain herself.

"First, I need to make a call to Henry Peyton. Stay in the bedroom and listen to what I tell him. After that, I'll tell you everything. It will all work out."

Brad dialed Henry and got right through to him. "Henry, this is Brad Lindstrom." After a few pleasantries were exchanged, he got down to the task at hand. "Henry, I want you to call off the dogs. I want to call a general meeting for the employees, and at that meeting, I will tell you and your clients everything that they want to know about the gold mine operation, and I will invite you to inspect the buildings and the mine and ask any questions that you may have. You can expect truthful answers to every question. This can't wait another day. I am suspending the aluminum plant operations tomorrow so that the employees will not be inconvenienced by having to meet in the evening. I want everyone to attend, including any past employees. Put the word out for me. Let's get this deal done without any more delay. The employees deserve it."

Henry agreed to put out the word and said that he appreciated the candor. "I'll see you tomorrow then, at 8:30 in the morning in the auditorium."

Brad reconstructed the entire day for his wife. He didn't leave out a thing. He knew that if he did, Kathleen would just keep pelting him with questions until she squeezed it all out of him. She didn't like the part about not telling who the good guy was, but she knew that this would be as good as it could get.

"You know that you left the impression with Henry Peyton that they wouldn't find anything unusual at the gold mine. Boy, are they all going to be shocked. You'd better have a doctor and an ambulance waiting outside … just in case."

"I want you there, and you are a nurse, after all."

"I'm not a cardiac care nurse, Brad!" Kathleen was pleased and felt relieved that it was almost over. She still was not used to the idea that Brad was sharing in the blame, but the more that she thought about it, the more she realized that their true friends at church and in town knew what type of man Brad was and that he would not be yoked together with his two brothers.

The Day Before

Henry Peyton's world had just suffered an earthquake. He could only imagine the embarrassment that he would soon feel. Henry jumped right to the 'worst case scenario' faster than a September hornet tormenting the kids on a Montana playground.

Henry wondered who would want to make a fool out of himself in front of his hundreds of clients and just about everyone else that he knew. He took the bait and swallowed the hook, the line, the pole and the fisherman along with it.

"Motherlode!" He screamed for the second time in two days. "You set me up, and now you're going to watch me squirm." The worst part was that he didn't know who 'mother lode' was. He suspected that maybe it was one of the Lindstroms, but he couldn't prove it. Henry had been pushing them pretty hard, and they seemed likely to want to hurt him the most. Brad's voice reminded him of "motherlodes," but it wasn't a sure match. It could be anyone who was familiar with the sale, and that was about everyone within a hundred miles.

If someone wanted to ruin his life, they could at least have the courage to stand up and attack from the front. This coward was more like a vandal, attacking from the shadows and leaving no tracks.

Henry put out the word about the meeting at the aluminum plant to the employees as best he could. He then picked up the phone and paused to take a deep breath before phoning Judge Costa. The judge came on the line with what she thought was good news. "Hi Henry, I've got your injunction right here. Boy, are you impatient? How do you want me—" Henry cut her sentence short and told her about what had just transpired.

"I think I was had. Tomorrow, we will know for sure. Keep the injunction under wraps until after a meeting that has been scheduled for the morning. Supposedly, the Lindstrom brothers are going to let us look everything over and answer any questions that we have. We might not want to use it after that. Maybe we can at least save you from destroying your reputation." Henry caught his breath and waited for a response. "It sounds like they either have nothing to hide, or else they're going to confess to everything that you suspect."

"You and I both know which way this one is heading. The Lindstroms, at least John and Michael, would never play fair with the employees if a large sum of money were involved. They either have nothing to hide, and I was set up, or they have succeeded in moving valuable ores or other assets offsite to a place that we can't touch."

They both suffered through a long pause before Henry spoke again.

"You're gonna miss a great 'tap dancing' demonstration tomorrow morning." Henry commiserated with the judge.

"I think I'll be there; after all, this case will show up in my courtroom soon enough if something funny is going on." The judge didn't try to guess what would happen at the meeting, but she sure didn't want to miss it.

Henry went home to create a list of questions to ask in the morning. He had most of them in his head already. Now, he would tone them down a little and not be so antagonistic.

After dinner, he noticed that a paid announcement was aired on the television, and his wife told him about a radio announcement that she had heard earlier describing the meeting. "Just what I need: 100% turnout for my crow-eating spectacle."

* * * * * *

The Blue Moon bar was filled with aluminum plant workers that night. Since the plant was going to be shut down for the meeting in the morning, it seemed like a great excuse for some blue-collar recreation. With only one bartender and two cocktail waitresses working on a typical weeknight, service would be a little slower than usual.

Country music and some good line dancing went on non-stop until 2:00 a.m. After that, the younger ones moved the party out to the parking lot for a little old-fashioned fighting. In Montana society, a night at the Blue Moon was like the symphony—the ballet and athletic competition together on the same stage. The opera house had long been closed, but the entertainment was still available in bars and clubs throughout the valley.

By 3:00 a.m., almost every pickup truck would be back home for the night. The only ones left behind were those with drivers who'd had their keys taken away or were smart enough to ask for a ride home. The police rarely arrest the customers, especially during the week.

The Night Before

Kathleen and Brad had been working most of the night with the arrangements for the morning meeting. On its way up from Missoula was over 3,000 doughnuts and other assorted treats. Brad called two of the plant lunchroom workers and asked them to come in early to prepare a few hundred gallons of coffee and orange juice. Brad had heard about last night's turnout at the Blue Moon and wanted to be sure to have the coffee ready for those who needed it.

After thinking about Kathleen's suggestion to have a doctor on-site, Brad called Dr. Miller and asked him if he could attend the meeting without telling him why. Dr. Miller agreed to come in at 8:30 and stay for a couple of hours. Brad thanked him. He knew that he would get right to the point during tomorrow's meeting, and any cardiac victim who couldn't handle the thought of being rich would be promptly taken care of.

Brad invited a local investment counselor to attend the meeting and asked him if he would speak to the workers. Rex Stack agreed to come and speak to the workers about investing. Rex was a little perplexed at the timing and of his prospective clients. Most of his clients were from Whitefish Lake and Kalispell. Investment counseling for the local blue-collar workers was usually obtained from their local pickup truck salesman or from Billy at the local pawn shop. They both offered advice on financing, albeit from different ends of the financial spectrum.

Brad called Michael to see how he was doing. "I hope to see you in the morning, Michael. I think you'll be happy when it's over, and I think you'll be surprised at the response we receive. Everyone will be so happy with the money that they're getting that they will abandon any animosity; you'll see."

"I hope you're right, Brad. I'll be there and so will John. I just got off the phone with him. It should be standing room only tomorrow morning."

The Morning

The alarm clock went off while Brad was in the shower. He never used an alarm clock—it was purely for Kathleen's benefit. She rose and left the radio turned on to the local news station. She laughed to herself about the news that would be playing tomorrow at about this same time. Most of the workers would probably be sleeping in or too seriously hung over to hear the story that they were a part of. Only the more responsible ones would be getting up and going to work tomorrow.

Brad was singing a song that he'd heard in church the previous Sunday. They started including more modern songs in the 9:30 Sunday morning worship service about two years earlier. This new style came with the new pastor. He was younger than his predecessor by about twenty-five years. He was smart enough to make slow changes, but for some, any change was met with concern. The 8:00 service was still faithful to the old Scandinavian Lutheran style of slowly grinding down the devil with virtually the same order of service week after week. The 9:30 was more aggressively confronting evil with song after song and prayer after prayer. It had a much more enthusiastic congregation and attracted the youngest members of the church.

The song Brad was singing was about Jonah from the Old Testament. Jonah wanted to go one direction and God wanted him to go another. Jonah ran away from God and ended up in the mouth of a whale. It all ends happily when Jonah sees the error of his ways and does what God wants him to do. Brad liked this song. He knew it took courage to do what's right, and sometimes you need someone's help to bring it to the surface.

Brad would always say that God saved his brothers from going to jail and suffering hell on earth for their mistakes. He was still worried about whether they would be saved for eternity.

He kept singing the song, trying to remember the words and notes. It was all pretty entertaining to Kathleen. She couldn't hold it in anymore and burst out laughing in the bathroom as Brad was turning the water off in the shower.

"Honey, I love ya! We'll keep sitting in the second pew in church—that's a promise."

For 15 years, Brad and Kathleen had always sat in the second pew. Brad liked it up there and always said it was because no one ever sat in the first pew. This allowed him to sing in his usual off-key style that wouldn't offend anyone else. He was fond of saying that if he were to sit in the back, the church elders would ask him to leave.

This was going to be a great morning. Brad likened it to telling a thousand people that they had won the Irish Sweepstakes and were instant millionaires. What fun this was gonna be!

John and Michael were thinking mostly about themselves and what would be left of their reputations, but even the most hardened heart would respond to the happiness of those people and join in on the celebration.

Michael was wondering what would happen to the local economy. The events that would be taking place were by far the strangest things that could happen to a town. Over 500 people would become multi-millionaires.

Hungry Horse, Montana, would be the richest city in the world per capita, bar none. Not even the oil-rich Middle East could boast of such wealth spreading among the citizens of one town.

How would Hungry Horse change? What kind of people would it attract now? How long would it take for the first millionaires to lose it all? What would happen to the people who never worked at the plant and wouldn't be reaping the riches? How would friends treat each other? What would they think about the Lindstroms?

Too many questions without answers for the time being. Someone would make a movie about this; they'd just have to.

Brad dressed, and Kathleen jumped in the shower. She sang a song too, but it was different. It sounded beautiful. She was blessed with a voice that could make you cry when she was singing an Irish ballad. Today, she wouldn't be singing any melancholy songs. The congregation knew she had the best voice in church. When Brad and Kathleen sang together in the second pew, they both made the congregants cry, but for very different reasons!

Brad and Kathleen met up downstairs in the kitchen to eat breakfast. When they said 'grace' that morning, it developed into more than asking thanks for their food. The prayer started with thanks and quickly turned into praise to God—praise for sorting out the predicament that greed had created.

They got in the car and drove to the plant. Both seemed to notice their surroundings in a new light. They lived in such a beautiful place. Surrounded by mountain peaks, the Flathead Valley stretched for over seventy miles. It was named after the Flathead Indians that had inhabited the area centuries before the first permanent settlers arrived in the 1860s. Lewis and Clark were the first 'white men' to arrive in the area in 1805 and encounter the Flatheads. The famous Hudson Bay Company traded with them for beaver pelts, and eventually, bison hide coats. According to other tribes, the Flatheads got their names because, according to legend, they would bind the heads of their young to flatten them. If you ask the tribal members, they will deny the validity of that story and insist that the name came from the sign language description of their tribe that placed both hands flat against the head. Their language was known as Salish, and that is the name by which they preferred to be called.

They accepted their new neighbors and eagerly traded with them. To the south and in the middle of the valley was the largest natural freshwater lake west of the Mississippi River. Flathead Lake was fed by the three forks of the Flathead River. To the north was Glacier National Park and the Canadian border. They lived in a natural paradise that they sometimes took for granted, but never for long.

7:00 a.m.

The beauty of their drive to the plant was interrupted by the sheer size of the aluminum operation. The steam and smokestacks had been idled since midnight when the last shift shut down. The plant was closed today and was nearly silent. Not since the early 70s, when the economy took a dive, was the plant operation as quiet as this. They entered through the main gate and waved to old Tom, the security guard. Tom started with the plant in 1957 and had guarded the entrance for twenty-eight years. Tom was a rich man in his home and family life; now he was a multi-millionaire, too. Brad drove in through the gate, slowed to a stop and then backed up to Tom's guard shack while rolling down his window.

"Tom, I want you to know that I appreciate you and your work for the company. I can always count on you, and I'm sorry that I haven't said it more often."

Tom quickly stepped out from his guard house and approached Brad's open window.

"Thank you, Mr. Lindstrom; thank you very much. I want to thank you for giving me a job for the last twenty-eight years, and I'm sorry I never told you that."

Tom and Brad looked at each other with a new respect. As they shook hands and looked into each other's eyes, Brad saw the man's face light up. As Brad drove off, he heard Tom whistling a happy tune.

"Why didn't I ever do that before? Look at what those words did to him, Kathleen. That simple gesture changed his whole morning—and mine too."

Kathleen and Brad went into his office. Kathleen didn't come into the plant very often but always enjoyed looking at Brad's other 'home'. When they were first married, Brad spent a lot of time in this office and on the road. Sometimes, Kathleen felt that their marriage life was a stepchild to Brad's business life. Those feelings slowly melted away as each year passed, and each anniversary brought her more happiness and more attention from Brad.

It was 7:30, and in an hour the auditorium would be filled with Glacier Mining Company employees and other interested parties. Brad told Tom to let in anyone who wanted to attend.

Brad knew what he was going to tell them and didn't need to make any notes. This would be from his heart, and he didn't want to break eye contact with the crowd even once.

Kathleen kissed Brad and went on ahead to the lunchroom to offer her help to the ladies that were preparing the coffee and laying out the pastries. He needed to be alone now, and Kathleen needed some busy work to calm her down.

She'd worked at the plant for ten years and knew most of the 'old timers'. The hair nets and white kitchen garb would soon be a thing of the past for these ladies. Kathleen was so happy for them that she could barely contain herself. All three tried to find out what the meeting was about, but Kathleen did not say a word. Sensing some concern that maybe the news would be bad, she said that they shouldn't worry and that they would be pleased with the outcome. This put them at ease.

Brad's brothers had arrived and were with him in his office. He put his arms around them to reassure them. He was glad that they were there.

The parking lot was starting to fill up now and Brad suggested that the two of them direct the people into the lunchroom for the coffee and pastries. Brad still needed a little more time alone, and John and Michael knew when they weren't wanted.

"Don't say a word about the subject of the meeting. Just reassure them that everything is okay." Brad admonished them as they left.

"How can we tell them what you are going to say, when we aren't sure ourselves?" Michael knew what Brad was going to say, but he didn't know how he was going to present it to the workers.

"You know what I'm going to tell them Michael."

It was 8:00 a.m. now, and about a hundred people were already in the auditorium and lunchroom. Michael and John took their places at the doors to the auditorium and directed everyone into the lunchroom for coffee and pastries.

Almost everyone asked what the meeting was about and John and Michael wouldn't budge. They did as Brad wanted and simply told them that this would be the best meeting that they ever attended.

"Is the sale still on?!" Were the first words out of everyone's mouth.

"The sale is on," they repeated over and over as the question was asked. Michael enjoyed seeing some of the retired workers that had been gone for years. He wished he could tell them right there that they were millionaires, and he genuinely was happy for them. John was always at the gold mine and hardly knew or even remembered most of them, but he, too, was getting into the spirit and was just as happy for them. The brothers hoped that they would still be happy with them after Brad gave his talk. It was 8:15 now, and the auditorium was filled mostly with older workers and retirees. Slowly, the younger workers began filing in. Kathleen noticed that a lot of the older workers looked in better shape than some of the younger ones. The last group to arrive were the ones who'd visited the Blue Moon the night before. This group sat in the back, sipping their coffee and complaining about headaches and hangovers. They wondered how long the meeting would take and when they could go back home to their beds. Little did they know—not one of them would be leaving this meeting early.

As 8:30 approached, everyone in the lunchroom cleared out and went into the auditorium. They were all in their seats and talking to each other, trying to guess why they were there. Most thought that it was just an informational meeting regarding the sale of The Glacier Mining Company.

Henry Peyton was there, too. He obviously had a bad night and looked like it. He felt rather stupid that he didn't have a clue what was going to take place, other than some questions being answered—answers that he was sure he wouldn't like.

Judge Costa sat in the back and intentionally didn't sit next to Henry. It wouldn't look good that the judge involved in a company dispute would be sitting next to counsel for the employees, and besides, she didn't want to be within range of Henry's misery. The judge thought that Henry was wrong to worry; she felt that he had found something and would be vindicated.

Two newspaper reporters were there, and a television reporter was present for the one station that the valley was able to support. The cameraman and television reporter were the same person, and he was setting up a tripod and a video camera. Just another boring meeting that would probably not even be aired. He would later say that he was glad that he had on his shirt and tie for the biggest story that he would ever break. He didn't know it now, but he would be on the national news at 6:30, telling his story to most of America. After five years of covering high school sports, snowstorms and county fairs, Pat Gould would get his 15 minutes of fame.

It was standing room only, and the mood was electrifying. People were looking around the room and when they saw who was there and how many, they knew it was big. The noise level surpassed the sound of the Great Northern Railroad's diesel locomotives that streamed into the plant yard, whistles blowing, and cars overflowing with aluminum ore.

No one was in any other part of the plant. Even the phones weren't answered. The gates were left open by Tom, who had been asked by Brad to attend the meeting.

Kathleen took her seat with the lunchroom ladies and other old friends and waited with the same excitement as everyone else.

John and Michael had walked back to Brad's office, and seeing that he was praying, they waited for him to finish. Brad left his office, and the brothers joined him for the short trip to the auditorium.

It was now 8:29, and the huge auditorium clock was at the center of attention.

8:30 a.m.

The three brothers walked onto the stage, where three chairs had been set up next to the lectern. John and Michael sat down, and Brad walked to the front of the stage, grabbed the microphone, and began his talk.

"Thirty years ago, we all saw each other for the first time. I'm going to talk about that in a moment, but first, everything's progressing smoothly with the sale, and I know that some of you were worried that it would be delayed while attorneys were acting as they do. What I am about to tell you this morning should probably have waited until after we closed on the sale of the aluminum plant and most of you had received your profit-sharing checks, many in excess of $100,000. I'll explain that later, though." A sigh of relief was heard throughout the room as Brad continued with his confession.

The only one feeling no relief was Henry. Now, he was sure that they wouldn't find any hidden assets, and his worst nightmare as a lawyer was becoming a reality.

"All of you signed up for a profit-sharing plan that wasn't what many of you expected it would be. Your wages over the last thirty years were never more than the national average for mine workers. Most of you started working for us back in 1955 when you were in your 20s and 30s; some of you were teenagers. As the 30-year anniversary ticks closer, almost 400 of you will be retired. Some in the last few years, but most of you will say goodbye to the Glacier Mining Company this fall. You will be the ones receiving the lion's share of the profits from the sale."

Brad was calmly setting the stage for the bombshell.

"$100,000 won't make any of you rich, especially after taxes, but it certainly is better than a gold watch and a retirement party at the Elks Club. What I am about to tell you will change your life a lot more than $100,000 would."

"After the first meeting in this auditorium in which most of you signed on with the company, Michael and I left the building and went home. We telephoned John later that evening and told him about the contracts that we had signed with you. He informed us that he had earlier that evening discovered gold in Teakettle Mountain. The discovery was incredible. John told us that he discovered a vein that was bigger than any previous discovery in North America. I think he described it as the size of a battleship. He sealed the mine when he left, and that entrance has been sealed ever since."

Henry Peyton immediately understood the implications and jumped from his seat as if to ask a question. Since his question had just been answered, he sat back down from his humorous reflexive action.

Judge Costa was smiling and was glad for Henry and for the employees. She knew where this talk was heading, and she was relieved for everyone.

Brad continued. "We had quite a heated conversation about the gold and about whether our new employees were entitled to share in one half of the 'mother lode.' "

Henry immediately knew who his source was for the clues to the gold mine. It was the same 'mother lode' that he spoke with on the phone two days before. Brad had spoken the name in exactly the same way that he did now. Brad was the 'mother lode' that had spilled the beans on his two brothers.

"We all have equal votes in this company now as we did back then. I am ashamed to tell you that two of us voted to separate the gold from the profit-sharing plan and keep it a secret. Some time ago though, we had a change of heart and we all decided that it should be shared and not kept from you. This morning, the jig is up, and we are all here to tell you everything." Brad paused, looked around the room and located Henry.

"Looking over at Henry Peyton, I can tell that there are a lot of questions. I hope to answer them all now, but if you still have any when I'm finished, we will truthfully answer them all for you."

Henry was pleased that the mysterious 'mother lode' had acknowledged him. Judge Costa was right. Henry was vindicated.

Doc Miller knew why he had been asked to be here. The gold must have been worth hundreds of millions, and these workers were about to find out what their share would be. Some of the older ones might not be able to handle the news; at the very least, some would faint.

Brad was getting to the good part and he started picking up steam. "I will tell you now that we intend to share the gold with all of you as if it were a part of the original profit-sharing plan. My only concern with telling you this now and not until after the sale of the plant is because when you find out the value of the gold and figure out your own personal share, I suspect that most of you will not work another day of your life for someone else. This will be of great distress to the new owners. Because of this, I am asking that you continue working until we find a reasonable number of new employees to fill your positions. I am also asking that we all show up for work tomorrow and keep the Glacier Mining Company operating."

Pat Gould stood motionless behind his video camera and checked it four times to make sure that it was recording properly. This story would be running statewide. He started making notes for his commentary that would wrap up the story.

Rex Stack now knew why he had been asked to be here. In the room were a number of wealthy people who didn't have any experience in handling large sums of money. He would be more than happy to assist them.

John, and especially Michael, were ecstatic with the way Brad was explaining everything.

Brad looked for Kathleen and found her in the back with the lunchroom ladies. She gave him the 'thumbs up,' and he winked at her before continuing.

"Before I get to the fun part, I would like a show of hands from those of you whom we can count on to be here tomorrow morning when the gates are opened."

Everyone in the room raised his hand; even Henry held his up before he realized that he didn't work at the plant. "I am truly gratified that you all will make that commitment."

Brad walked over to his brothers to gauge their response. They were both elated that they were here to witness Brad's brilliance.

"How many of you have worked here for more than a year but fewer than two? Please raise your hands." Brad looked around the room and saw about 20 hands go up. "Congratulations, your share of the gold will be approximately $118,000, plus another $3,500, more or less, from the aluminum plant sale. Not a bad bonus for a year's work. See you all here tomorrow, I trust." Brad said this with a huge grin, but he was serious, and they knew it.

The audience exploded into one loud cacophony of a thousand voices. The ones that were good at math were able to figure out their share—those were the ones who screamed the loudest. The ones who had trouble with numbers were just as happy; they knew they'd be getting a lot—they just didn't know how much.

Brad yelled into the microphone and asked the crowd to hold it down for a minute. "Those of you who have worked here for ten years, raise your hands." More hands were raised.

"Congratulations to you all. You are millionaires. Your share of the gold is worth somewhere around $1.2 million and about $35,000 from the profit sharing." I know I'll see you all here tomorrow, right?"

Kathleen had raised her hand. Until now, she hadn't really thought about her tenure at the plant or that she would be sharing in the gold.

"How many of you have been here since we opened the doors back in 1955? Show me your hands." Almost 400 hands were raised.

"A big congratulations to those of you who started with us and stayed with us through thick and thin. Your share of the gold will be about $3.5 million, and an additional $104,000 from the sale of the aluminum plant. Remember, the first shift is at 7:00 a.m. for those of you who have not yet retired."

The place went wild. Pat Gould's television camera was knocked over, and he scrambled to retrieve it. Everyone was yelling and screaming. Henry Peyton, Judge Costa, Rex Stack and anyone else who didn't work at the plant realized that these blue-collar workers were worth a lot more than they had been just yesterday. The natural order of the valley was turned upside down, and they were now at the bottom.

Old Mr. Inkvist fainted, and Doc Miller rushed to his aid with smelling salts. Mr. Inkvist started work on the first day that the plant opened. He came to and was back in his seat, doing fine. So far, so good, he thought.

Brad let the crowd continue in their celebration. He couldn't have quieted them down anyway. He went over to his brothers and asked them to stand with him at the front of the stage. The three brothers were glad that it was almost over, but they still had one more thing to do.

After about five minutes, Brad picked up the microphone and asked everyone to be seated.

"I want to ask you all something." Brad waited for the room to become quiet.

"I hope that you will forgive us for what we did." The three of them stood together and seemed to look into the eyes of everyone there. The employees began to clap their hands and stand. Soon, the entire room was standing and applauding the brothers. Brad was so humbled by their forgiveness that he began to cry. He wiped his tears with the handkerchief from his breast pocket and remained facing the people that they had almost cheated. John and Michael couldn't look at them now and held their heads down. That picture said it all to most of the workers and everyone else in the room. They knew what type of person Brad was, and now they saw his courage and character shining brightly. Most felt that their fortunes had been in Brad's hands and he was the brother who didn't want to hide the gold from them. Brad came to their rescue and did the right thing.

"Thank you," was all he could say.

"I'll answer any questions that you may have now, and when we are finished, I would like to ask Rex Stack to come up to the stage and talk about money management for a few minutes. I asked him to be here today as a friend and as someone to help you get on the right track. He is not here to sign up new clients. He didn't know why I asked him here until just now, and Rex, I apologize for putting you on the spot."

Rex was taken aback. He was being asked to stand and speak in front of over 500 millionaires who didn't have any idea of how to handle large sums of money. He scrambled to find a notepad from his briefcase and began outlining a class on 'Investment 101.'

"And now, if you have any questions?" Brad asked as his two brothers left the center stage and retreated to their seats.

Henry Peyton jumped up and was recognized by Brad, who motioned for him to come up and speak into a microphone.

"Before I ask any questions, I would first like to thank the three of you for your candor and honesty. You know that I was retained to represent the workers in the sale of the aluminum plant. I may not speak for everyone here, but I forgive you and respect you for your courage in standing before this group and doing the right thing."

The applause broke out again, and after it settled down, Henry resumed speaking.

"I guess I do speak for everyone here."

Henry began his questioning. "Could you tell us how much gold is in Teakettle Mountain?"

"We estimate the value to be over $ 4.5 billion dollars."

"How do you know what it is worth until you actually mine it and process it?" Henry was asking the questions that everyone had been thinking, but like a family reading the will of a long-lost relative, nobody wanted to come right out and ask how much was in it for them.

"The gold has been mined and processed. It is neatly stacked in the mine shaft and contains over 12,500 ingots of pure gold, each ingot weighing approximately 50 pounds. By the current spot market rates, that puts the value well over $4 billion.

Henry was shocked by this revelation. "How did you do it without anyone knowing about it?"

"It was done over 30 years. The gold was in a huge vein which made it easy to get to. It was processed at night and poured into ingots and stacked in a hidden shaft in the mine."

"What's the next step?"

"The first thing we should do is to secure the mine to protect the ingots. The gold should be moved into the gold processing plant and weighed, tested for purity, and inventoried. After that's done, we will sell the gold and distribute checks to the employees based upon each person's pro rata share. This much gold will certainly have an impact on world gold prices, and we should expect a certain amount of fluctuation in value."

The big question that everybody wanted to ask was Henry's next question. "When should the employees expect to receive their share of the gold proceeds?"

"I don't know much about the gold brokerage business, but I would expect that in about two weeks, we should be able to pay the employees."

This is what everyone wanted to hear. The town of Hungry Horse had just won the lottery and all that was left to do was to cash in their tickets and pick up the money.

"I have one more question for you. I know I have been hogging the microphone." Henry had hundreds of other questions to ask, but they could wait.

"How will this affect the sale of the aluminum plant?"

"It won't if we are able to keep the plant operating. I know that it is tempting to quit work and not show up, but that wouldn't be fair to the buyers. We have got to keep coming to work until replacements are found for those of you who would like to retire. I know it won't be easy for a lot of you, but I again ask you to help us all out. It is possible that the buyers may back out. They would stand to lose over 30 million dollars. It's not a likely scenario, but it is possible."

Brad appreciated Henry's last question. It was for Brad's benefit, and he knew it.

Pat Gould was standing next in line behind Henry and was glad that Henry was finished and he would have a chance to ask a few questions. Most of the good ones had already been asked, but he had a few of his own.

"Mr. Lindstrom, I'm Pat Gould from the local NBC affiliate." Brad knew who Pat was, as did everybody else in the room.

"Yes, Pat."

"Could you tell us who the lone advocate for the employees was when the three of you voted whether to conceal the gold or not?"

"The three of us agreed not to divulge the results of that meeting, and I certainly will keep my word."

Pat asked another question. "When did you decide to end the concealment and to tell everyone the truth?"

"I am not here to disclose any information regarding our private discussions and decision to share the gold. As I told you earlier, two of us felt that the new employees of the aluminum plant had no rights to the gold, and one of us disagreed. The timing of when two of us changed our minds and agreed to share the gold is not important. The gold is intact and has never been moved. At no time has any of the gold from Teakettle Mountain been sold. You can draw your own conclusions as to whether it was decided yesterday or almost 30 years ago."

"I guess it must have been decided a long time ago, since the gold has not been touched. I can see now why you wouldn't want to disclose it. It would have probably shut down your pride and joy, the aluminum plant. Is that why you had reservations about disclosing it before the sale of the plant?" Pat was desperately trying to get something for his news broadcast.

"Move on, Pat; we're finished with this line of questioning."

John and Michael were able to lift their heads a little higher now. Pat had reached the conclusion that the decision to share the gold with the employees was reached years ago, and the reason for not telling anyone was to protect the Glacier Mining Company from having all of their employees quit at the same time. If Pat had come to this conclusion, they hoped that everyone else would, too.

Pat had another one. "Are you concerned about what will happen to this community and the employees' ability to handle this unbelievable wealth?"

"I certainly am. That's why I asked Rex Stack to come here today." Brad looked back at where Rex was sitting. "Have you figured out what you're going to say to these people, Rex?"

"Not yet, Mr. Lindstrom. I hope everyone has a lot of questions for you."

The employees all laughed at Rex being put on the spot. Most were glad that he was there and that he might be able to put everything into perspective for them. They all knew who he was from his radio ads and financial advice column in the newspaper.

To Rex's relief, the questioning went on for another half hour, and when there were no more, Brad asked him to come up to the stage.

"Ladies and gentlemen, I would like to introduce Rex Stack."

Rex was surprised at the round of applause that he received. Had he been asked to speak at the plant last year, he was sure that everyone would head for the doors. Not this morning.

"Thank you, Mr. Lindstrom. I have been sitting in the back trying to think of something to say to you about the huge amount of money that you will soon receive, and the only advice I can give you right now is not to put it in your mattress; besides, it won't fit."

Laughter erupted, and this put Rex at ease. Since that joke worked, he decided to go for another.

"How many of you here are Democrats?" Almost two-thirds raised their hands. "You won't be after the taxes are deducted."

This one got some laughter, but not as much as the first joke. Rex decided to end the jokes and get down to business.

"Invest your money and keep the principal intact. With the numbers that I heard this morning, the interest from a quality investment could be ten times what you are currently making at the plant. Find a good investment counselor and listen to their advice. Check them out thoroughly and examine their track record. Don't put it all into one basket. Spread it over a few different people to minimize the risk."

Rex went on for about ten more minutes, giving the group a primer on investing. He talked about everything from charitable giving to loaning money. He told them to be ready for an onslaught of friends and family asking for money. When he was finished, he was pleased with the attention that they gave him and was impressed with their many questions.

Brad thanked Rex and closed the meeting with a prayer from his pastor, who asked for wisdom, compassion and forgiveness. He asked that everyone would be blessed with their gift from God; to be good stewards of that money, and to use some of it to serve others less fortunate. It was a brief message but covered a lot of ground.

"See you in church this Sunday," Pastor Ingraham said as he walked off the stage.

"I guess you will be able to put that new carpet in the sanctuary now, Pastor. Let's see, ten percent of $4 billion should get you a nice pad with it, too."

The pastor tried to give Brad a look of displeasure after that last comment, but he couldn't even come close. He knew that his church had quite a few members in the auditorium, and his church would be receiving a windfall, too. Truth be told, he was as excited as everyone else.

Brad thanked everyone for coming and wished them happiness and a nice day off.

"One last thing. You all know that I have always had an open-door policy to my office on Fridays to talk about anything you wanted to, except money and your love life. The door is still open for you, and I want to amend the policy by allowing you to talk about money now all you want. Your love lives are still off-limits, though!"

The meeting closed with them all laughing at the last sentence.

Brad walked over to his brothers, and they all embraced, glad that it was all over. Henry Peyton walked up to Brad and thanked him and then his brothers.

"Let's go to my office for a few minutes and work out a few logistics," Brad said, taking charge.

"I'll station Tom and another guard at the mine right away, and we'll get a few more in there for around-the-clock protection. If you would like to send in some of your own people to make sure everything is secure, let me know, and I will see to it that they will have total access."

Brad asked John and Michael to go to the gold mine to make sure that it was protected until the guards were all in place. Henry said that a meeting with Brad could wait, but asked if he could go with the brothers to the mine. Michael told him to follow him there in his own car.

Brad left the stage and waded through the crowd. No one was leaving—most were still in shock. He found Kathleen at the back and walked toward her as everyone either shook his hand or patted him on the back.

Kathleen hugged him with everything her small size could manage. As they were walking out of the building, Margie, the head receptionist for the last eighteen years, said that she would man the phones for the day and be in again first thing in the morning.

He saw Tom enlisting a guard to remain at the aluminum plant while he went over to the gold mine.

Pat Gould was fumbling with his video camera and was trying to set up the viewfinder to include the entrance to the plant with the Glacier Mining Company sign over the doors. It was comical to see him start the tape rolling and then run in front of the camera to give his commentary on everything that had just taken place. This story was going to play around the world, and he could barely contain himself.

"We sure have a lot of good people in this plant, Kathleen."

"I know, Brad."

Relief

Brad and Kathleen got in the car and just sat there for a while. Both were glad that it was over with and were happy to be going home. Soon, the world would hear about Hungry Horse, and the media would be descending upon the valley in force.

They both sensed that the money would be a double-edged sword for a lot of the people and that concerned them. For now, though, they wouldn't try to guess what the future would reveal.

The socio-economics of the valley had just been totally gutted. Hungry Horse was not just the wealthiest community in the valley— it was the wealthiest in the world. This had a chilling effect on Brad. This little town of 1,500 residents had more money per capita than anywhere and it would be studied for years by scores of anthropologists and psychiatrists and everything else in between.

"Your brothers must be pleased with the way everything turned out," Kathleen said, breaking the quiet. "You must be, too."

Brad should be happy with everything. He told the truth and that ended it all. John and Michael weren't going to jail, the employees got what they deserved and whatever concerns they had about saving face were dashed.

Something didn't seem right though, and he couldn't put his finger on it. Something sinister was omnipresent. Something that started this morning. Like a chasm in the Earth that people fell into, he felt that the money had opened up a portal for something evil to enter into the hearts of the good people of Hungry Horse.

"Brad, did you hear me?"

"Sorry, honey, of course I'm pleased. I'm just tired and worried for the employees, worried how the money will affect them and this valley."

"Let's go home and change our clothes and go for a hike in Glacier Park. We'll go up to Avalanche Lake."

"I'd like that, Brad. We'll bring our lunch and spend the day."

The Treasure State

The news spread quickly. On the drive back from Glacier National Park, Brad and Kathleen's serenity was pierced by the radio news broadcasts that described the meeting and the mayhem that shook the valley.

Kathleen turned off the radio and looked at Brad. "Welcome back to reality!"

Brad was glad that she turned it off right away. He would see it all on the evening news soon enough.

They pulled into the Conoco gas station to fill up the car. As Brad walked inside to pay, he noticed the newspaper stand with the two-inch headline that you couldn't miss:

We're Rich!

Two words summed it all up.

Melinda was at the counter, and she saw Brad walking through the door.

"Mr. Lindstrom, you sure turned this town upside down. I can't believe it. It's so weird! Yesterday, folks were complaining about my gas prices, and now half the people who bought gas could buy the whole damn station if they had a mind to. I'm worried for the younger ones and what they'll do when they get a pile of money. It's gonna get interesting around here!"

Brad paid for the gas and agreed with her. "Time will tell, Melinda. Time will tell."

Brad put a quarter into the newspaper stand, took out a paper, brought it out to the car and handed it over to Kathleen.

"Save this for your scrapbook. Today is the dividing line between the past and the future of Hungry Horse. In years to come, historians will be describing the Valley in terms of the "Pre-Gold" and "Post-Gold" eras.

Brad drove home while Kathleen read the paper. Her favorite part was the interviews with the new millionaires.

"What are you going to do with the money?" Was the obvious question that they all were asked. Some grappled with it, while others knew the answer right away.

"Pay off my mortgage and pay all my bills, and then just breathe for a while."

"Buy a new truck for me and a new convertible for my wife."

"My youngest daughter can go to college now. She's been working hard to save enough for the tuition. She won't have to anymore."

"I'm quitting my job at the plant as soon as the sale goes through."

"I just don't know."

"I'm taking my wife on a Caribbean cruise … after I pay a lot of bills."

"Proposing to someone I should have married three years ago. I hope she'll say 'yes.' I've got a feeling she will."

"Retiring in style."

"Selling my trailer and building a new house."

"Invest."

"Give 10% to my church. We can burn the mortgage and fix the roof."

"Take the vacation of a lifetime."

The paper quoted over 50 people. Each one had his own idea of what to do when he got his money. Some thought about how the money could be used to help others, but most thought about themselves.

Like most people in Hungry Horse, they had spent their lives living on the edge. Now, they had breathing room for the first time, and it felt pretty good. Most thought that money would change from something that you got on Friday and was spent before the next paycheck into "fun tickets" that could bring security and happiness.

Brad pulled into the driveway and put the car in the garage. He noticed a bunch of notes on the front door as he drove in. Kathleen heard the phone ringing and rushed into the house to answer it.

"It's some guy from Newsweek. He wants to talk with you."

"Take a message." Brad wasn't ready for his fifteen minutes of fame.

Kathleen hung up after taking the name and number and looked at the digital dial on the answering machine. Over seventy-two messages had been recorded.

Brad turned on the TV while Kathleen took the phone off the hook and started transcribing all of the messages. The local news was about to start.

"I wonder what the lead story will be?" Brad looked over and winked at Kathleen, who was not enjoying her task.

"The girls' high school basketball state tournament over in Libby," Kathleen remarked—and she would have been correct on a 'normal' news day.

The newscast began. Pat Gould was standing at the entrance of the Glacier Mining Company, holding a microphone.

"Over 500 people became instant millionaires this morning in Hungry Horse."

The scene changed to the auditorium meeting earlier that morning. All the excitement and screaming was captured for the viewers.

"Stay tuned for Newscenter 4."

The girls' state basketball tournament news would have to wait until later in the broadcast.

The opening of the news show dissolved into the big story. Pat Gould recapped his 'story of a lifetime' for the audience and actually did a pretty good job.

Kathleen stopped taking down the messages when a shot of Brad standing on the platform telling those with their hands raised that they were millionaires came on the screen. She was one of the people with a hand raised.

The story had a life of its own and Pat was just hanging on for the ride. He could have filled an entire newscast with interviews he'd conducted with the instant millionaires.

Pat continued with the amazing story. "The Lindstrom brothers kept the gold a secret for three decades and didn't want to tell the employees because they knew that everyone would quit and cripple the aluminum plant. As the gold was running out, they decided to sell the plant, and tell the employees about the gold when the sale of the mining company was complete. When rumors of the gold began to spread, they decided that it couldn't wait any longer. Fears that everybody would quit working and shut down the aluminum plant gave way to pressure from attorneys that had suspected something unusual was hidden in Teakettle Mountain."

The scene changed from the Glacier Mining Company plant entrance, to the entrance of a mine shaft opening on the back side of Teakettle Mountain.

From there the camera bounced its way through the shaft until it came upon a wooden door that opened into a black void. The lights were turned on and the shimmering reflection played havoc with the aperture of the camera lens. Pat quickly adjusted the camera.

There it was! A stack of gold as tall as a man that could fill a room. It was breathtaking. Brad had not seen the gold before and this was truly incredible. He laughed when he saw that the gold had been stacked into three piles just as Michael had asked him to do it. One half of the gold was neatly stacked and separated from two other stacks. Each of the two smaller stacks was about a fourth of the total. The gold was all on pallets and the forklift that made the dividing of the gold possible by one man sat off to the side.

Kathleen wondered if the brothers would each keep a quarter of the gold for themselves and not give any to Brad. She wondered if they would continue to do the right thing or slip back into the greed trap that had snared them 30 years ago. She had thought about it a few times since the meeting but didn't want to mention it to Brad yet.

As Brad looked at the gold, he wondered the same thing. Brad had signed off on his share of the gold and he was prepared to live by it. He didn't want to be a part of the scheme and he certainly wasn't going to ask his brothers for his share. Brad meant what he said. The fact that he signed his name to a document was irrelevant. Any decent attorney could get that letter nullified in a hurry. But Brad's word was as good as gold, and to him, that was even more valuable.

The newscast changed from the treasure to a group of employees who had gathered around Pat and his camera. Their answers to Pat's questions about what they would do with all the money were that same as the newspaper's. Brad recognized most of the people as they gave their answers. The camera captured the excitement much more than the newspaper could have.

The television station broke for commercials and Kathleen came over to the big, overstuffed chair and sat on Brad's lap.

"So far, all of the messages are from friends and the media. John and Michael each left a message and both thanked you for what you did. You should call your brothers after the news." She looked over the names of the various callers and reeled them off for Brad: "Henry Peyton, Rex Stack, Pastor Ingraham, Pat Gould, and oh yes, the attorney for the aluminum plant buyers."

"That will be an interesting conversation. They've got to be a little nervous." Brad didn't relish that call.

The newscast returned and finished with an abbreviated weather report and, of course, coverage of the girls' basketball state tournament over in Libby. Hungry Horse lost their game. Four of the starters were now daughters of millionaires. The coach blamed the loss on the distraction created by the gold, but he really didn't care about the loss that much. His parents both worked at the plant and he learned earlier that day that they would be taking home over $5 million themselves.

Like most of the children of the new millionaires, the coach thought about his inheritance for the first time in his life.

Those who were only children thought about it more than the children from the larger families. Most would be motivated to help them conserve their windfall and others would be helping them spend it on 'toys' for their parents—toys that they could play with, too.

Legal issues surfaced and became important to a large group of people. Suddenly the phrase 'Last Will And Testament' had new meaning to potential heirs. The effect of the gold was trickling down to the next generation. Family reunions were taking place throughout the valley.

Those who had moved away were burning the phone lines to share in the excitement. After the national newscasters broadcast the story, children across the country who hadn't called home in years would be phoning their parents.

Ex-wives and husbands would soon be heard from. They would want to have their share, too. The gold would also turn out to be a windfall for the attorneys.

Every employee who was single was experiencing a sudden surge of popularity. The older ones were more attractive than the young ones; after all, they had the most money.

Marriage proposals were on the minds of these gold diggers. A good prenuptial agreement would reduce their ranks in a hurry.

Brad and Kathleen refocused on the television as the national news blinked onto the screen. They watched as the opening of the show began. Tom Brokaw's lead story was about the valley.

"Tonight we bring you a story about the wealthiest city in America. It's not about Beverly Hills, California, Grosse Pointe, Michigan, or Palm Beach, Florida. It's about a small town that you've never heard of and it's located in a most unlikely place: Montana, the 'Treasure State'.

We now go live to Hungry Horse, Montana, where Pat Gould from our local NBC affiliate has this exciting story."

The screen was filled with the worn-out sign boasting that Hungry Horse was the 'best dam town' in America. The sign faded to the Glacier Mining Company offices. Pat Gould was standing at the main entrance and the same video that had played 30 minutes earlier on the local news was now being broadcast nationally. Although most of his video was edited down to about four minutes, it was still a show stopper.

Tom Brokaw's face appeared on half of the screen with a live picture of Pat Gould on the other. Pat was on the 6:30 national news that was actually broadcast two hours earlier on the East Coast. The two-hour time difference made this a tape of the original 'live' broadcast that aired earlier.

"Pat, according to our research, Hungry Horse, Montana is now the wealthiest town per capita in the world. How are the people reacting to the news?" Pat was on national television for the first time in his life. The live broadcast would test his mettle and he was up to the test.

"About five hours ago, more than 500 people learned that they were millionaires, most of them multi-millionaires. I don't need to tell you that the mood was one of pure joy."

Tom continued his questioning. "You've interviewed over forty of these new millionaires. What's the consensus? What are they going to do with all that money?"

"Their responses range from paying off their mortgages to buying a new truck, to taking a lot of vacations. Most all will retire from the plant and enjoy a life-style that is foreign to almost all of them." Pat was holding his own.

"Pat, I understand that about half of the residents will receive a small fortune, if not millions. How is the other half taking the news?"

"Tom, most of those who didn't work at the plant are genuinely happy for their friends and neighbors. With over four billion dollars that I've been told will be distributed in the next two weeks, most everyone will benefit from that kind of wealth being spread around."

"Thanks for giving us this story. I'm sure we will be following this one for quite a while. We have been talking live with Pat Gould in Hungry Horse, Montana. What a great story, Pat!"

"Thank you, Tom."

Brad switched over to CNN on his satellite dish and saw another reporter recapping the news about the gold. CNN was broadcast around the world and this story had wide appeal. There was something about winning the lottery, or coming into an unexpected fortune that always captivated the attention of everyone the world over.

Brad turned off the television and looked over the messages that Kathleen had given him. His first call would be to Jim Allcort, the attorney for the buyers.

Jim had left his office number and his cell phone number along with his home phone. Brad dialed his cell phone, and Jim answered.

"Jim, Brad Lindstrom here."

Jim asked a stream of questions and Brad answered them all. Jim wasn't pleased with what he was hearing and threatened to pull out of the deal. Brad knew that he wouldn't, three other suitors attempted to buy the plant, and Jim was sure that Brad would have no problem arranging another sale. Brad made it simple for him.

"Jim, if you don't want to go through with the deal, then don't. We certainly can't force you. The aluminum plant is a healthy and profitable operation; it stands on its own. Quite a few will be retiring and you will have to fill their positions. Almost four hundred would have retired anyway in the next year. That was certainly no surprise. Plenty of people are available to step in and keep things profitable.

I'm sorry for the distress that this is causing you, but we expect that you will go through with the purchase."

Jim threatened to reduce the sales price to reflect the changes. Brad let him blow off steam before wrapping up the conversation.

"The gold will not affect the operation. If you don't want to buy the plant, then don't. If you would like us to entertain a restructuring, fine—put it in writing and we will certainly consider it. Either way, please let us know promptly so that we may review our alternatives."

Jim really had no options. If he insisted on changing the deal, Lindstrom could refuse and keep the $24 million held in escrow. That amount, plus the $6 million spent on due diligence and other fees would put their 'walk away' cost at about thirty million dollars. Jim knew that it was still a viable and lucrative deal, and besides, the business plan for the buyers included some serious downsizing.

Brad ended the call by asking Jim to deal with the Lindstrom's attorneys regarding any changes that they might be seeking.

"How did it go?" Kathleen wanted to hear it all.

"What other choice does he have? We both know that it's still a great deal for them. They're using the gold to try to get some concessions from us. I got the feeling that he was just going through the motions to see if we would bite.

Most venture capitalists come in after a sale and slash and burn, starting with the employees. They're referred to as 'vulture capitalists' by those in the financial markets."

"Are you going to call the others?"

"Let's have dinner first. I'll call John and Michael now and deal with the others later."

Brad couldn't get through to either brother. Their lines were busy and, more than likely, off the hook, too. The Lindstroms would be hounded for days by the media. Brad didn't look forward to all of the hoopla and attention that was being forced on him.

Brad remembered the messages on the front door and went to take them down. Two were from reporters, and another was from Henry Peyton. Henry was concerned about the sale and had been contacted by Jim Allcort. Brad called him after dinner and assuaged his fears. Henry was smart enough to know that the deal would go through, but since the bulk of his firm's compensation was directly tied to a successful closing, he was a little nervous about the latest events.

The two had a peaceful dinner, thanks to having taken the phone off the hook. They relaxed in their bedroom, watching television and talking.

Brad was dozing off, and when he awoke to a loud commercial, he saw that Kathleen was asleep, so he turned off the TV. He began to pray for his employees and his brothers before thanking God for Kathleen.

They were both asleep by 10 o'clock but tossed all night thinking about what the next day would bring and wondering who would show up for work.

The Bad Moon

The place was packed. Charlotte had anticipated the crowd and called in reinforcements. She had owned the Blue Moon for almost 30 years and knew that tonight would be like no other. She asked two off-duty cops to come in and make their presence felt. The Flathead County Sheriff's Office stationed a patrol car in the parking lot for the entire night.

It was a good thing; alcohol mixed with money made a strange cocktail. It affected the customers in different ways. Some just enjoyed the night on the dance floor, while others exhibited arrogance and a new bravado that seemed to escalate with every sip of beer and bourbon.

Money gave some the courage to say things that never should have been said. The alcohol made them feel bulletproof. More than ten fights had broken out before nine o'clock. The cops broke them up swiftly. Tonight would bring jail time for some of them as the patience started wearing thin on the bouncers and police. For now at least, no one had been arrested.

The place was filled with available women. Most were dressed in their cowgirl best. From their cowboy hats down to their cowboy boots, they were looking mighty fine. They were all trolling for millionaires, and the boys didn't mind it a bit.

Most of the single ones that had trouble getting a date before the gold, confirmed their theories about money being the main reason that the women rejected them. For a few of them, however, the money didn't seem to help at all.

As the night wore on, the fights changed from those involving fellow workers and millionaires into boyfriends coming in and looking for their girlfriends who were attracted by the money. Those were the serious fights. By midnight, half a dozen had been arrested and hauled into the jail. It was getting worse by the hour.

By that time, the county sheriff had called in every available policeman in the valley. Disturbances were being called in so fast that it strained their resources as never before.

Every bar within a ten-mile radius was having trouble, and numerous cases of domestic abuse were pouring in. Just about every woman in a bad marriage who had turned down a wedding proposal from an aluminum plant worker felt cheated out of the gold and said so to their husbands.

At one o'clock, the sheriff shut down the Blue Moon and two other bars. The roads would soon be filled with drunk drivers.

After the Gold

The alarm went off at 5:30. Brad was in the shower. Kathleen listened to her radio and remembered her humorous thoughts yesterday morning about the gold being the main news story. It wasn't what she expected. The news wasn't about the gold, but about the effects it was having on the town's residents.

The jail was filled with hungover fighters and domestic abuse cases. Two partygoers had been killed in separate auto accidents. One irate boyfriend shot and killed his girlfriend, and a "family reunion" had ended when a man was stabbed three times in the chest.

"Brad!" Kathleen yelled. "It's terrible, what's happening!" She was stunned.

Brad quickly jumped out of the shower and found his wife in tears.

"The news is horrible. Two people were killed in car wrecks after the police shut down the Blue Moon and a few other bars. A man shot and killed his wife, and another man was stabbed at a party! The jails are filled with drunks and fighters."

Brad had feared something like this, but he didn't think that it would happen so fast or be accompanied by such violence. He was sure each incident was brought about by the gold. His previous worries were justified. The gold had been a source of evil from the beginning when his brothers were overtaken by greed. Now, it has been released by John and Michael and has spread throughout the community.

"I've got to get into the office and find out the names of the victims. You can come with me if you want to."

Kathleen wanted to get back into bed, as if she could pull up the covers, put the nightmare away and start the morning all over again.

"I'll stay here for now. Call me when you find out any-thing."

Brad dressed and headed downstairs.

"How about some breakfast?" Kathleen knew that he wouldn't be eating anything for a while.

"No thanks, honey. I'll call you as soon as I hear anything."

The drive into the office was punctuated with the news reports that listed the terrible toll that the gold had taken: three dead and one clinging to life in the hospital; a dozen domestic violence cases and a dozen more serious fights with injuries, all in the first twenty-four hours. Relationships were ripped apart, exposing an underbelly of greed, jealousy and pent-up emotions. This was unchecked evil, and it was released from that cold and dark shaft that hid the gold that had been excavated from Teakettle Mountain.

"It shouldn't be like this," Brad said aloud. He wondered why this newfound wealth couldn't make things better for people. Why couldn't they enjoy what God had given them and use the money to improve their lives and the lives of those around them.

He turned into the plant and stopped to speak with Tom. They both just shook their heads and tried to make sense of it all. Tom told Brad that he knew two of the victims. One was a Bobby Thompson, killed while driving drunk. Bobby had worked at the plant for thirteen years. The other was Melissa Fredrich, shot by her ex-husband over a fight about the money. Melissa had been a secretary at the plant for over sixteen years. Brad knew them both.

Tom went on to list the names of two other plant workers who were hospitalized and suffering from wounds sustained while fighting. Brad could barely speak, and Tom was in even worse shape.

"Thanks for coming in this morning, Tom. Please call my office if you hear any other news." Before Brad pulled away from the guard shack, he asked Tom to lower the flags to half-staff. Tom liked that idea a lot.

Brad was the first one in the office and was glad that he was alone. He needed to cry and pray for the families and friends of the victims.

Brad remembered to call Kathleen, and he told her what he had heard from Tom. She knew Mellisa well and broke down. She didn't know Bobby, but had worked with his mother at the plant when she was a staff nurse. Brad didn't want to talk about it anymore, and Kathleen understood.

They hung up, and both promised to relay any new information as they heard it.

In almost 30 years of work at the plant, not one person died on the job. There were a few serious injuries over the years, but no one was killed.

Brad could hear people arriving at work and gathering in the break room. Most had just heard the latest and were either crying or just staring in disbelief. Brad left the solitude of his office and went out to join the others.

"Mr. Lindstrom, have you heard?" Margie the head receptionist, true to her word, showed up for work.

"Yes, Margie. Tom told me about Mellisa and Bobby Thompson. I don't want to believe that it's true."

"The other accident victim was Ron Wagoner. He drove his truck into a ditch and flipped it over near LaSalle. He'd been drinking all night up at the Sportsman Bar."

Ron had been a foreman in the main processing plant for over twenty years.

"What about Irene? Was she with him?" Brad had always enjoyed Ron and his wife, Irene. Ron was always in a good mood, and it was infectious.

"No, thank God. She was home with the grandkids. His oldest son was with him, but he was wearing a seat belt, and although he's in the hospital with some broken bones, he'll be out in a few days."

Brad couldn't take much more of this. He decided to keep the plant closed until next week.

"Margie, I need you to call Tom for me and tell him to get everyone back into the auditorium. We won't be opening up production until after the funerals."

It was Friday, and the thought of trying to focus on work was now out of the question. Brad needed to talk with everyone again, this time to tell them the bad news and to give them all some advice—sort of a mass group therapy session mixed with a plea for sanity.

Michael arrived and went straight into Brad's office. "Can you believe this? It's like this town went crazy last night. We all need to regroup and realize that we're not bulletproof. We miscalculated the downside that sudden wealth would inflict on some of our workers. I'm glad that you decided to keep the plant closed."

"Thanks for coming in early. I tried to call you last night, Michael, but your phone was busy."

"I took it off the hook after an hour of endless calls. I suspect you did the same. I drove by and saw the messages on your door and figured you and Kathleen were in hiding."

"We went up into Glacier Park and hiked up to Avalanche. Kathleen counted over seventy messages on our machine. John left a message too, but his line was busy when I tried to call him."

Michael quietly closed the door to Brad's office and sat facing him in the small seating area next to the window.

"He came over to my place for dinner last night. I guess we were hiding out, too. We both just wanted to say thanks again for what you did yesterday. After dinner, John and I decided to tear up the letter agreement we all signed earlier this week. John had it in his safe deposit box. We both are ashamed for what we did and for what we tried to do. I hope that you will forgive me for my part in all of it."

"Michael, you know that I love you and that I forgive you. No strings attached. I also want you to understand that I appreciate that you and John decided to tear up the agreement, but I don't want any of the proceeds from the gold. Frankly, it frightens me. You've seen what it can do. Just look at the broken lives that it left behind after less than 24 hours after the announcement was made. These people don't even have the money yet! What will happen after they get their checks?"

"We're different from them, Brad. We've been wealthy most of our lives."

"I don't think that we are that much different. I don't want to find out that we are all the same deep down. It's a gamble that I'm not ready or willing to take.

Michael didn't expect this response to their 'generous offer' of the money.

Brad didn't, either. Maybe if the events of the last night had been different, he would have accepted it. Now Brad felt that the offer was motivated by guilt and as payment for a job well done on the auditorium stage yesterday.

There was a knock on the door, and John peeked in.

"Come on in, John." Michael moved over to the couch and motioned for John to sit in the chair that he'd vacated.

"Hi guys." John's tone summed everything up. "It's terrible. I couldn't believe what happened. It reminds me of one of those European soccer clubs winning the World Cup and then watching their 'overjoyed fans' destroy the stadium and city. I'm dumbfounded."

"Brad ordered the plant closed until after the funerals; I agree with him. We've got to shake some sense into this madness." Michael meant every word.

"I didn't really know any of the victims, but I'm sure both of you did. I'm truly sorry for them and their families. I am not good at dealing with this sort of pain. What are we going to do?" Helping people wasn't one of John's strengths.

"When I drove in, Tom told me that you want to assemble everyone in the auditorium. What's your plan?" John's method of dealing with everything in his life always started with a 'plan' of some type.

Brad didn't have a 'plan.' He detested the way John used that word. All he knew was that the employees needed to stop and learn something from the horrible wreckage that was strewn all over the valley. Like the NTSB, after a plane crash, they would have to assemble the pieces of the wreck to understand how to prevent it from happening again.

This assessment would have to be done quickly before the carnage resumed. The next 'plane crash' would probably occur again when the gold was sold and the checks were distributed.

"I just feel the need to get us all together in the same room and circle our wagons. I can't help feeling responsible for the damage caused by the gold. We need to accept the past and be prepared for the future together." Brad wanted to be there with the workers, share the sadness and let them know that he cared.

"I think you're being way too hard on yourself, Brad. Is that why you won't accept your share of the gold?" Michael's statement caught John off guard. John looked over at Michael and was totally confused.

"What do you mean?" John looked at Brad in amazement.

"Michael told me that the two of you decided to tear up the agreement and share the gold with me. I was humbled by your offer, but as I told Michael, I can't accept it."

"Give it to charity, then." John didn't get it; his world was filled with gray areas. Brad's was black and white. "Give it to your church and let them use it for good."

"God doesn't need me to finance him. The only debt he owes is to his believers—a debt that I expect to redeem one day."

Brad wished that he hadn't said it quite so harshly. "I'm sorry John, I don't mean to come off--"

"It's my fault, Brad, we are different and I admire you for your steadiness. My faults are highlighted almost as much as your qualities are whenever we speak. I hope you will forgive me for the gold scheme and for my lack of understanding of your position. I'm jealous. You have such an inner peace and a clear direction in your life. You are truly a happy and contented person and I wish I had some of whatever it is that you have."

"I'll preach to you later. Let's go down to the auditorium and join the others."

Brad wasn't kidding. His brothers' lack of faith was an issue that had been haunting him. They weren't getting any younger, and their lives didn't have any purpose. His leadership style had obviously gotten his brothers' attention, and now was the time for a more direct approach.

Direction

Brad guessed that only about half of the workers showed up for work. Most were standing in groups talking about last night's events; some were sitting and staring. These people needed some direction.

The three brothers entered the auditorium and slowly worked their way toward the front. Brad and Michael stopped along the way to commiserate with the employees. John looked like a lost lamb. He hadn't taken the time over the last thirty years to get to know anyone at the plant, and he followed his brothers around the room like a newborn duckling following its mother from one pond to another.

Half of the people had shown up for work without hearing about the preceding night's fury. Everyone was touched by the death and violence that occurred. They were experiencing a variety of emotions. The ones that heard the news before arriving at work were starting to deal with it in their own ways: sorrow, shock and shame for their community. Yesterday, Hungry Horse was the toast of the world and now it was devastated by human nature. Although most wouldn't say it, they cared about what the world thought about them. Yesterday they felt special and loved by the attention that the media had given them. The media would be back, and nobody wanted to answer the questions that they would be asked now. Now their dirty laundry was hanging on the laundry line, instead of their Sunday best that they'd worn just the day before.

Brad sat on the front of the stage and asked everyone to sit down. He recapped the news and names that he heard about for those who didn't have all of the details. It seemed to open the wounds all over again. Some broke into tears, and others preferred to hug or hold hands. Brad asked that a moment of silence be observed for the victims that they knew about and for the ones that they didn't.

After the short quiet that seemed like an hour, Brad asked them to pray with him.

"Dear Father, we asked you to extend your awesome hand to the families and friends of the fallen. We ask you to give us the ability to forgive those who have done wrong and to help all of us shoulder the pain and loss that is being felt through our valley and beyond. We ask that your healing touch be felt by those who are suffering."

"Let us learn from our mistakes and do those things that will glorify you and not ourselves. Help us all to realize our gifts—the gifts that you have given us to use and to share with others. Help us to be good stewards of the earthly treasures that you have given to us in the past and that you will be given to us in the next month. Let us rebuke the greed that is all around us, so that we may identify it and help us to understand it and recognize where it comes from. Let us acknowledge that it is an evil that we are helpless to fight without your love and guidance. Tame our arrogance and deflate our boasting. We all want to do the good things that would bring a smile to our faces. Please give us the courage and the wisdom to do so. In your name, we pray, Amen."

Brad sat down next to his brothers and asked them if they would like to say anything. John said no, and Michael didn't have anything to add.

Brad told the employees that the plant wouldn't be reopening until after the funeral services had been performed.

"I don't expect that we will be processing ore until a week from this Monday. Please plan on returning then. We will need some yard volunteers to offload the train cars that are stacking up."

George Olney stood up and offered to put a crew together and keep the yard clear.

Margie volunteered to keep the phones operating during the week that the plant would be closed.

"I can't thank you two enough. I appreciate your concern and loyalty." Brad was touched that they cared enough to pitch in.

"We need to talk about all that has happened and how we can prevent more of the same. I am very concerned for all of us as events unfold during the next month. I don't have any answers, but maybe some of you do. I'm asking for your help and would appreciate any suggestions."

Susan Clossen stood up after it became apparent that no one had offered any magical solutions.

"I don't know what to tell you about how we can deal with what has already happened. I hope that most of the steam has been blown off and that things will calm down." Susan was more worried about the future than the past.

"A lot of us don't know what we're going to do with the money when we receive it. I fear that my husband and I will make mistakes and be taken advantage of. I know of people who fear legal claims to the money from ex-husbands and wives. Maybe we should turn the focus from what we are going to buy with the money to how we should be good stewards, as you put it."

Susan spoke for most of the people in the room when she continued.

"We need to talk with professionals to help us plan for the future and to guide us through the jungle. Jeanette's husband works at the bank, and she told me that only $100,000 is insured. If the bank were to fail, anything that I had on deposit over that amount might be lost."

"What about taxes? Are they deducted before we are paid, or are we responsible for paying them? We all have hundreds of questions and no idea where to find the answers."

Brad stood up and proposed an idea.

"What if the Glacier Mining Company were to line up a cast of professionals to answer your questions? We could bring in accountants, attorneys, financial planners, and family counselors. We'll set up shop right here in the auditorium. I'll ask for volunteers in our community to come in and sit down with you. We can fight your fears with knowledge and help to arm you with straight-forward advice. What do you all think?"

"I would like that, Mr. Lindstrom, thanks."

Susan sat down, and Brad asked if anyone else would like to speak. Nobody else came forward. Brad was surprised that not one of them wanted help in dealing with the loss of their friends and coworkers; the focus was still on the money that would be coming into their lives. He gave them the benefit of the doubt and wrote it off as the individualism that was a trademark of Montanans. Personal problems to them were exactly that—personal. The thought of talking with a psychologist or, heaven forbid, a psychiatrist was the ultimate sign of weakness to these people. Leave the shrinks to the screwed-up New Yorkers and Californians who really need them.

"Would anyone be interested in talking with one of the pastors from our community?" Brad thought that idea might be more easily digested than the prospect of sitting with someone from the mental health care field.

About forty hands went up.

"I'll ask some of the clergy to be here also."

The response to his last question raised Brad's hope for employees. He noticed that most of those raising their hands weren't regular churchgoers. Maybe meeting with local pastors on 'neutral turf' would open their hearts and minds to learning about spiritual things, and maybe that would fill a place in their lives that needed attention—soon!

Brad asked if anyone would like to say a few words for Mellisa, Bobby or Ron. Margie stood up to speak about Mellisa.

"I worked with Mellisa for over sixteen years. We both started here about the same time. I was at her wedding and babysat for her two kids. She was a dear friend who suffered through a failing marriage. She was always optimistic and never had a bad word for anyone—even her ex-husband. I know that Mellisa is in heaven, and that reward is greater than any that she could receive here on Earth. Her children are now orphans. They will receive her inheritance, though—an inheritance worth more than gold or money. Her spirit will live on through them and will last longer than anything else that they will receive."

Margie started to cry and sat down. She had more to say, but she couldn't compose herself.

After a few minutes had passed, Terry Matthews stood up. After wiping away his tears, he spoke of his friend, Bobby Thompson.

"Bobby was my best friend, and I will miss him. He worked his entire life at the plant and was always a bright spot for me. Bobby could always make me laugh. He didn't deserve to die the way he did last night. He hadn't taken a drink of alcohol in over fifteen years. I can't understand what made him do it last night."

Brad knew that it was the gold that killed him. He had dealt with too many alcoholics at the plant to remember. They'd all had a 'reason' for drinking. Some would use it to cover pain, some would use it to celebrate, and some to escape the sense of hopelessness that they felt. Bobby fell back into the trap of addiction because he was weakened by a false sense of security—a security made of gold that he believed would take care of all of his troubles. When it came time to test the strength of that 'security blanket,' he used his Ford pickup and twelve shots of bourbon. All three of them pierced through the blurry veil at sixty miles per hour. Behind that thin blanket was lurking a telephone pole.

Terry was breaking down but was able to continue. "Bobby's momma is in my prayers. I hope that she will find the strength to get through this week and months and years ahead. He was her life, and he was my buddy."

The room was filled with the sounds of muffled crying as Terry sat down in his chair.

Brad stood up and remembered Ron.

"Ron Wagoner was always smiling. It didn't matter to him what day it was, how gloomy the weather was, or what pressure he was under. He was always smiling and it infected everyone that he worked with—especially me. He was looking forward to retiring with his wife Irene and enjoying his family. He was always talking about his grandkids. I don't know why he had a bumper sticker on his truck that read, 'Ask me about my grandkids.' Nobody had to ask him about his grandchildren to get him to tell you how great they were."

"When we prayed earlier and asked God to help us fight greed and evil, I wasn't thinking about Ron.

Ron was a giver. He was always thinking of others, especially those who weren't as fortunate as he was. Ron would have been an even greater example to all of us as we receive our windfall from God and search for ways to use it. He would have shown us how to be good stewards and custodians. He made a terrible mistake last night—a mistake that cheated us out of his smile and his friendship. A terrible mistake that cheated his wife, his family and his friends."

"I know that it's hard to make sense out of Ron's death. In our sorrow and confusion, we sometimes try to blame something or someone. It's easy to point a finger at God and challenge his wisdom, but that won't bring back Ron. It's a greater mistake to try to anticipate what God's plan is for each of us and second-guess him."

"I'm sorry for the preaching. I'll quit and leave it to our pastors and priests. I would like to thank God for giving us Ron and ask him to send more like him. We need people like Ron to help give our journey purpose."

Brad sat down and prayed for the families again. They all would need a lot of prayer to get them over this hurdle and to get them over all the other hurdles that were coming their way.

About seven or eight others spoke for the victims. When it became apparent that no one else was going to stand up and speak, Brad rose.

"Let's all go home now and comfort those who aren't here this morning. I'll make the arrangements to have this auditorium filled on Monday and throughout the week with people to answer the questions that many of you have. We'll place an announcement in the paper. Look for it on Sunday morning. Now go take care of yourselves and your families."

Brad, Michael and John left the auditorium and went back into Brad's office. Margie stopped them and offered to handle the announcement in the paper. Brad smiled at her and dictated the words as she stood at the door.

"Don't call it in until I tell you, Margie. Thanks again." Brad asked his brothers to draft a list of professionals that they could ask to come in and help the employees and their families. Brad did the same, and they compared the names. The three of them settled on a list. Each began calling the names on their list, and within half an hour, they had the auditorium staffed for the week.

Brad called Margie on the intercom and finalized the announcement that would run all week in the local paper, starting on Sunday and running each day, ending on Friday.

Brad tried to return the stack of business calls on his desk. His first call was to Kathleen. Michael went to his office to catch up on his own work. John, true to form, went over to the gold mine to check on the gold and oversee the inventory and transport of the ingots into the building next to the mine.

Home Again

Brad left the office around five and drove home. The latest news on the radio brought more pain. The stabbing victim was Logen Kennedy, and he died from his wounds sometime after lunch. Logen started at the plant in 1957 and was murdered by his son. Kathleen heard about Logen but decided not to call Brad at the office. What good would it do? He would find out soon enough.

Brad came in through the garage door and dropped into his big chair in front of the television. Kathleen brought him a glass of orange juice and told him about Logen. He turned on the television and waited for the 6 o'clock news. He didn't want to, but felt that he had to watch it.

Tonight's broadcast would be a difficult experience for both of them. They turned their attention to the TV screen as the opening teaser came on. It was a shot of the flag in front of the plant at half-mast. Pat Gould came on the screen.

"Triumph turned into tragedy as Hungry Horse prepares to bury four of its own."

Pat recited the statistics and circumstances of the night before. The local news provided pictures of wrecked cars and wrecked lives for all to see. Brad turned down the volume. The rest of the broadcast centered on the happiness of the day before turning into chaos and sorrow. Ron Wagoner was one of the people that Pat interviewed the day before. Ron looked exuberant during the interview, and he talked about the new freedom that he and his family had now that their worries were over. The pictures of his demolished car were a shocking testimony to the frailty of each of us.

When the local news ended, Brad turned the sound on, and they both listened to the national news. Tom Brokaw came back on, and again, the lead story was from Hungry Horse. The tenor of tonight's broadcast was a complete turnaround from last night's show.

"What happens to a town when 500 people discover that they are millionaires?" The picture changed to the flag at half-mast. Brokaw continued his dialogue. "Violence, murder and death."

Brad had to turn off the TV. He didn't want to witness his small town's character being annihilated on national television. It was a good thing that he did. The story would go on to portray Hungry Horse and the workers at the aluminum plant as a town populated by immature idiots who went crazy. The rest of the world was led to believe that Hungry Horse was far too inept to handle the millions of dollars that each of the workers were to receive, and the broadcast was filled with pictures of the accident victims and the vehicles that two of them died in. Pictures of the dead from happier days were shown as if to mock them for what had happened. Hungry Horse was no longer the innocent little Montana town filled with happy new millionaires. Now it was a laughing stock that would be providing hours of 'news entertainment' for the nation and the world to smirk at.

Pat Gould wasn't included in this night's broadcast. NBC had flown in its own national reporter and cameraman. Pat was told that it would be more balanced and that he was too close to the people involved. Evidently, Pat wasn't good enough for NBC because he wouldn't oversensitize the tragedy.

All the networks were in town with their own crews doing the same hatchet job that NBC was. USA Today would feature a cover story on Hungry Horse. It would be on the newsstands in the morning. If the death and destruction wouldn't bring the residents of the valley to their knees, then the shame of living there certainly would give it a shot.

The residents of Kalispell and Whitefish Lake were having fun with the tragedy of Hungry Horse. This confirmed to them that they were better because they assumed that they would never act like the blue-collar workers of the aluminum plant. They were just jealous though, and as some people attempted to build themselves up by tearing down the lives of others, so did many of those who were not sharing in the wealth. 'I told you so' was repeated over and over again amongst this group of spoiled sports.

For the first time ever, Brad wanted to just get away from it all. He wished that the gold was sold, that everyone got their money, and that he and Kathleen could enjoy their retirement. He would never desert Hungry Horse, and he knew it down deep. He would stick it out and help his workers get over the hump. He was smart enough to realize that he couldn't hold everyone's hand, but he sure could try to help.

Twenty-Two Days

Twenty-two days. That's how long it took to sell the gold. The checks would be distributed in the morning. The funerals were over and the injured were all back home.

The residents were licking their wounds and the distraction of the money that they would get in the morning made most forget about the last three and a half weeks.

Over 400 employees took advantage of the professionals that the brothers had lined up for them in the auditorium and Brad was pleased with the response. He had a strange and unwelcome feeling that once the money was distributed, a new chaos would ensue.

The sale of the plant was back on track with a scheduled sales date sixty days out. That money would just be a little icing on the cake compared with the checks that would be handed out in the morning.

The media was back in town again, poking fun at the people of Hungry Horse. They had become a national pastime and the public was well positioned by the media to expect more sensational stories as these hopeless country bumpkins from Montana would be transformed into the 'Beverly Hillbillies' of the '80s.

Forbes and Fortune magazines were in town to get a share of the 'sitcom' of Hungry Horse printed on their pages. This story sold a lot of papers and magazines.

Brokerage houses and investment counselors, schemers and scammers from across the country were calling every phone number listed in the book. Some people, including Brad, were receiving twenty and thirty calls a day at their homes. Brad added an unlisted line to his home and left the original one to be answered by his machine. Even that didn't work, though. Automated calling software was being used to dial every conceivable combination under the single Hungry Horse exchange, and the more industrious cold callers were getting through.

Boats, cars, trucks, jewels, furniture, hunting rifles and shotguns, hot tubs and Jacuzzis, furs, and anything else that would fall under the category of adult 'toys' were in the valley and waiting for the barrage of impulse buyers that were poised and ready to attack. The best restaurants had plenty of expensive French champagne chilled and waiting for the hundreds of celebrations that would be taking place. If you hadn't made a reservation by now, you didn't stand a chance at getting a table at any decent restaurant. Of course, a discreet $100 bill placed in the right hands would make it a lot easier for a nice table to be found.

Most of the workers were showing up on time, and Brad and Michael were filling the anticipated vacancies. The plant had hired over 200 new employees and was in the midst of training them. They were working closely with the new buyers, and it became apparent that they intended to trim almost 300 positions at the plant. This worked out well for everybody. Jim Allcort's earlier complaints were just a smoke screen to try and whittle down the selling price of the plant. It was unsuccessful.

Henry Peyton was happy that the sale was on track, but he was overwhelmed with legal work, mostly on behalf of the former spouses of aluminum plant workers. Seven women and four men had the 'courage,' bolstered by a nice chunk of money, to begin the process of obtaining a divorce. Henry wasn't the type to try and help them fix what was obviously broken, but to his credit, he referred them to counselors and clergy and let them have a whack at it. Two couples agreed to try and work things out.

Over twenty new marriages were in the works—some the culmination of years of courting, and some the by-product of overnight greed and lust. The younger ones seemed more responsible than some of the older ones. A few of the more 'mature' and older fellows surely needed a well-placed kick in their pants.

A joke was going around town about two men in their seventies talking about one of their upcoming weddings. When the friend found out that his buddy was marrying a beautiful 23-year-old girl, he was shocked and asked him if he had lied about his age.

"Yes, I did," he replied with a smirk. "I told her I was in my nineties!" His answer summed up a few of the more hastily planned weddings in the valley. This joke was a direct jab at Billy Porter. When his wife died four years ago, he said that he would never remarry. Billy would be getting a check for about $3.5 million, and that was all that 23-year-old Brandy Johnson needed to know about him. The fact that he had a weak heart was a bonus.

Michael and John talked a lot about Brad's refusal to take his 'share' of the money. They both agreed to keep it for him, and they flipped a coin to decide who would hold it. John called tails, and tails it was. The money would be under John's care until Brad came around to his senses.

Kathleen would be receiving more than a million herself, and she teased Brad about her 'mad money,' which she called it.

There were a few worrisome, anonymous threats directed at the brothers from some disgruntled ex-employees who were fired in the early fifties. They reasoned that if they hadn't been fired, they would have still been working at the plant and getting a share of the treasure. Brad turned over a couple of letters to the police, but nothing ever came out of the threats. Michael had done most of the hiring and firing back then, but didn't remember anything out of the ordinary.

Tomorrow's headline from the local Hungry Horse paper was ready to go. It would be another two-words, about an inch and a half tall. 'Brace Yourselves' was all it said. It seemed appropriate. The Hungry Horse News won a Pulitzer Prize in 1964 when Mel Ruder covered the big flood. He never won a second one, even though this story had massive international appeal.

The entire valley was waiting for the checks to be handed out. The new millionaires wanted it for the fun and happiness that they thought it would bring and all the others wanted them dispersed so that they could enjoy the entertainment value that it would certainly bring to the valley. Almost two and a half billion 'fun tickets' were on their way to the past and present workers, with an equal amount to be divided ostensibly among the three brothers.

The Federal Reserve was prepared for the onslaught, and the Hungry Horse Bank, which handled the plant's account, already had the money on deposit. Federal Regulators were swarming around the bank, checking them out like never before. They passed inspection, but the Feds left four employees on site to monitor things. No one minded a little government intrusion... except for maybe the bank.

Real estate prices soared. More people listed their homes for sale in two weeks than had been sold in the last three years. The prices were getting ridiculous, but that didn't slow down interest in the properties a bit. People who never considered selling their homes tried their hands at making a little killing in the real estate market. 'It's not for sale' quickly changed into 'make me an offer.'

Some of the kids were acting as if they were getting the money instead of their parents. This brought on a few problems in the schools. This was mostly confined to the high school, but even a few of the kids in the elementary school were affected by the money and were trying to out-brag each other. Every child seemed to know how much money their parents were coming into, and that changed the pecking order in the schools.

Things were still kind of crazy, but at least people weren't dying or exhibiting the violence that had threatened to destroy the delicate fabric of the community just a few weeks ago. Tomorrow would be a big test for Hungry Horse. Hopefully, it would pass this latest one.

The Big Day

Brad awoke two hours before Kathleen's alarm clock. He couldn't sleep. He was downstairs watching CNN on his satellite. The top news stories included Hungry Horse. It seemed like everyone in the country had their eye on the small town. No one wanted to miss the next installment of the 'poor little millionaires' mini-series that had been on the news for over three weeks. The next chapter was not to be missed.

Two national networks were already at work on their own mini-series about the town. The script was being written daily as the facts and fables filtered down out of the valley. Rumors were rampant about these shows. Kathleen kidded Brad about who would play his character. She thought Robert Redford would be perfect. Brad reminded her that Redford would be too expensive for the networks, and besides, Brad said that he was much better looking than Robert.

Brad changed the channels on his dish and stumbled on a documentary about children in Africa who were starving from the drought that had been plaguing the entire continent for the past three years. It broke his heart. He was going to do something about it. He didn't know how or when, but he was sure he could help some of them. Brad turned off the television and began to pray. He couldn't get those pictures of the little children with the distended stomachs out of his mind. He prayed for those children who were starving in Africa and for all the hungry children around the world. He prayed for his employees who were starving for purpose and direction in life. He prayed for restraint and calm in his community.

He stopped praying, and with his eyes closed, he tilted back in his recliner and listened and waited for God's guidance. As usual, it wasn't coming. He didn't know what to expect when it would come, but he was sure that it would, sooner or later.

He had been in his chair, lying perfectly still for over an hour, when he heard the alarm upstairs. The radio was on, and the subject was about what else, the big day that everyone was waiting for.

"I'm downstairs, honey."

"Everything okay?" Kathleen had been worried for Brad ever since she learned about the gold.

"Yeah, I couldn't sleep, so I came down here instead of bothering you."

They dressed and had a light breakfast before going to work. Brad was surprised when Kathleen asked if they should take both cars or ride together. He had forgotten that a check was waiting for her, too, and she wanted to come in and pick it up.

"Let's take both. I've got a lot of work to do. Have you decided what you're going to do with all that money?" Kathleen smiled at Brad. "I've got a few ideas. The first thing I'm doing is take 10% off the top as a donation to our church. It'll be fun to write a check for $120,000. I want to earmark it for the youth ministry."

Brad and Kathleen had been underwriting most of the church's projects and ministries for over ten years. About six years earlier, they had decided to tithe at least 10% a year. In fact, it had been more like 15%. That amount added up to over two million dollars over the previous ten years. The rural Lutheran Church was able to support over 15 missionaries and hundreds of other projects and ministries around the valley and around the world. With about thirty members of Brad and Kathleen's church picking up checks today, Pastor Ingraham would have an interesting deposit slip to fill out on Monday morning.

"You're the only one not picking up a check this morning." *How ironic*, thought Kathleen. "I can loan you some money if you're a little short today."

"Don't worry about me, honey. I'll be picking up $23 million in about 60 days!"

Kathleen followed Brad into the plant past nine remote video trucks from all the networks and major news corporations. The flag at the office was still at half-mast, by Brad's order. The new owners could raise it up if they wanted to; the current owners wouldn't.

Tom was at his post.

"How are you holding up, Tom?" Brad looked to his right and to his left at all the news trucks and antennas and swarms of reporters.

"Just fine, Mr. Lindstrom. They've been pretty polite so far. It looks like I won't have to rough any of them up."

Tom couldn't hurt anyone. He didn't weigh more than 120 pounds with his revolver strapped on. They both had a good laugh. He drove through the gates, and Kathleen followed him to the front of the office. A few cars were already in the lot. They could expect perfect attendance today. It was Friday, and Brad and his brothers decided to let them all go home after they picked up their checks. As usual, though, Tom and Margie would volunteer to stay on and 'hold down the fort.'

The two of them went inside Brad's office. Kathleen went into the break room and put on the coffee. She brought in a cup for herself and Brad and closed the door.

Brad opened the safe that was concealed by a wood panel and brought out a stack of over a thousand checks that would need his signature. The regular paychecks would be distributed at the same time. The signatures on those were machine stamps of Michael's moniker. Brad wanted to personally sign the profit-sharing ones.

As he signed each one, he looked at the amount and tried to visualize the face of each recipient. He couldn't place a face with *every* name, but he could for most. Kathleen attached a document to each check for the employees to sign. This had been drafted by the attorney for the aluminum plant. They would be signed by each employee before their check was handed over to them.

Copies had been distributed earlier in the week to Henry Peyton for his approval. It was a receipt for the check and an acknowledgment that it was payment in full for their portion of the gold proceeds.

"How's your wrist holding up?" Kathleen had a stack of signed checks about nine inches thick. He was halfway through them.

"I'll make it before the 8:30 'ceremony' in the auditorium."

"Here's one I don't know if I should sign." Brad held up Kathleen's check for $1,192,712.12.

"You'd better if you know what's good for you." He quickly signed her check.

"Sign the document and put the check in your purse if you want."

"Are you kidding? I want to wait. Don't even show it to me now. I'll walk up to the front and sign the receipt like everyone else. Where are the checks for your brothers?"

"They already have theirs in the bank. A little less than $1.25 billion each. We all signed off yesterday.

The attorneys were confused when they saw that I wasn't taking any of the money. They are legally sworn not to disclose it to anyone. They're still scratching their heads over that one. I'll bet my brothers are having fun moving money all over the place."

John would have surprised Brad. He was moving money around, all right. He had set up a charitable foundation in Brad and Kathleen's name and had already transferred over $830 million into its account. That amount was equal to 1/3 of the total earmarked for the three brothers. John and Michael would tell Brad later and ask him and Kathleen if they would act as co-directors. They could keep it under wraps for about six months at the longest. The foundation was less than 48 hours old, and it was now one of the largest in North America. John was sure that Brad wouldn't want to leave him at the helm.

Brad completed the signing of all of the checks, and Kathleen had them neatly organized in alphabetical order. Brad loaded them into a cardboard file transfer box and closed the lid.

"Do you need any more coffee?" Kathleen was heading out the door to get some water for herself.

"None for me honey, thanks." Brad sat at his desk and looked around his office. He had spent almost thirty years in this wood-paneled home-away-from-home. It looked like a men's club, with its dark paneling, deep green carpet, heavy walnut furniture and a desk set. Burgundy leather chairs and Charles Russell artwork were everywhere. The paintings and castings by Russell were quintessential Montana—horses and cowboys, framed and in bronze statues, were found on every wall and table. They didn't build offices like this anymore. Nowadays, drywall and drop ceilings with fluorescent lighting and commercial-grade carpeting are the standard. He was going to miss this place, especially the people who worked in the offices and the plant.

Kathleen stopped to talk with the girls and was caught up in the excitement of the office staff. Some tried to act casually about the profit-sharing checks, but they failed miserably. The moment someone showed any excitement, they all joined in like school kids. The conversations between employees over the last three weeks always contained a reference to their length of service. If someone wasn't sure, they would just come out and ask. It was the same as asking how much their check would be, but a bit more circumspect. Each year, the total was about $120,000, and the employees were expert mathematicians in totaling each other's shares.

Just like the schools, the pecking order was being rearranged. Some of the lowest-paid employees who had been there from the beginning were worth a lot more than some of the younger managers who were their bosses. Brad enjoyed that part the most.

Kathleen slipped away from the 'girls' and back into Brad's office. It was time to bring the checks to the auditorium.

He picked up the simple cardboard box that contained $2.5 billion in checks, and the two of them headed to the waiting workers.

"Are you coming, ladies?" Brad loved to tease the office staff.

"Just mail mine to me." Margie always loved to tease Brad right back.

The office staff fell in line behind Brad and Kathleen and followed the money trail to the packed auditorium. Many had to stand in the back and out in the hall. The mob cleared a path for Brad as Kathleen and the ladies stayed in the back. Everyone looked at the box. They suspected their checks were inside.

Brad walked up to the front and grabbed the microphone off the stand. It was turned on and ready to go. He set the box of checks on a table that had been set up for him.

"I'm sorry, but I don't have the checks with me." He paused for only a short time and said, "Kidding. They're on the table over there in that cardboard box."

That broke the ice. Laughter broke out, along with a lot of sighs of relief.

"The big day had finally arrived. I'm going to call you up in groups in alphabetical order to hand you your checks and the receipt document for you to sign. I'm afraid that you'll have to show me your ID badge before I can hand over the check. Lawyers orders, you know. A driver's license or other picture ID will be fine for those of you who have retired or don't work for us anymore. Any checks that have not been claimed will be placed into tonight's mail and dropped at the post office. We'll keep them here until 4 o'clock for the benefit of any latecomers."

They were all ready to come up and get their checks. It was all smiles and joking around for the workers that day.

"And by the way, we don't expect any of you to work today. When you sign the receipt and pick up your check, you can take the day off. I'm sure you all have something better to do anyway."

Michael and John worked their way up to the table and took up positions next to Brad. They were a little late, but it didn't matter to Brad or anyone else in the room.

"I'm going to call up groups by the first letter of your last name. When you come up, get your receipt document from John and sign it. Please produce your ID at that time and show it to Michael or me, even if we know you. We've gotta do it the way that the attorneys want it. Hand me the signed receipt, and I'll give you your check."

Kathleen laughed at the thought of showing Brad her identification.

"Here we go! Bring on the A's."

Fifty-three A's walked up to the front table. As they showed their IDs and signed the receipt, each was given a check. Some screamed, some laughed, some kissed the check ostentatiously and held it up high so that all could see. Brad had never kissed so many women at one time. He tried to sidestep the bear hugs and kisses, but gave up after his evasion tactics proved unsuccessful for the first ten of them. The media was allowed in and they were collecting their footage for the evening news. The employees were playing for the crowd and the cameras, and they loved it.

They brought their checks back to where their spouses, friends, or family were sitting and proudly showed them the biggest check that any of them had ever seen. When they filled out their deposit slips, they would notice for the first time that the slips didn't provide enough room for all of the numbers that were on the checks. The bankers wouldn't mind it, though.

It only took a couple of hours to get everyone their checks. Some stayed around for a while, but most left after a short time and headed to the bank. The lines were repeated over again as the Hungry Horse Bank was crediting more than two billion to the accounts of its customers. The little Hungry Horse Bank had more money on deposit than was at the Federal Reserve Branch that serviced the entire state.

Jim Holmes didn't trust banks; he wanted to cash his check and take the money home with him. It was a pretty humorous scene at the bank when he was told that they couldn't give him $3 million in cash. He raised such a ruckus that the Federal Reserve auditors had to explain to him that just because the bank didn't have millions of dollars in its vaults didn't mean that his check was no good. They explained that if he really wanted the cash, he would have to wait until next week. Jim deposited his check and got a receipt. He did walk out with ten thousand in cash and a promise to return on Tuesday to get the rest. That receipt just wasn't the same as having the cash to Jim. The manager made a note to call Brad and have him explain it all to Jim.

Over a thousand checks were in the hands of the past and present workers of the plant. With the weekend looming, Brad was worried about what would happen, and his thoughts wandered back to that night of carnage and havoc that had been well-documented by the media. He was not optimistic, even though a temporary air of restraint seemed to bring a shaky truce to the region.

Brad and Kathleen left the office around 4:00 and headed home to ride out the storm that both knew was intensifying on the horizon. Kathleen followed in her car.

The media had their latest story and was editing today's episode for the masses. Pat Gould was out of the national loop, and that was a shame. His take on the matter was more level-headed than the talk shows and newscasts that seemed to sensationalize everything totally out of proportion to anything that resembled reality.

Caveat Emptor

The stores and car dealerships were jammed with cash buyers. The parking lot at the plant would look like a new car lot on Monday—that is, if anyone showed up. So many cars and trucks were sold on Friday that some dealers looked like they had gone out of business. By sundown, there were simply no new cars and trucks available to buy and the lots and showrooms stripped bare of all inventory astounded their salespeople. The employees had so much money that they were not only buying cars and trucks for themselves, they were buying them for their spouses, children and parents.

The same was true with the RV lots—sold out of every camper and motorhome. They, too, looked like they were out of business.

The A&W drive-in restaurant was filled with new cars, and their happy owners ordered food and ice cream. The ones that couldn't get in because of the waiting line just drove around showing off their new machines.

The stores were busier than at Christmas. Everything that these wealthy shoppers wanted, they could now have. It was as if everyone's name was Jones, and they were all trying to keep up with each other.

The biggest frustration for most of them was the waiting time for getting their new toys. The more serious consumers had been shopping for weeks and had put things on layaway. Some car and truck buyers had picked their prizes out weeks in advance and had the paperwork waiting when they arrived at the dealers, checkbook in hand. Their vehicles were prepped and waiting to be picked up. No financing hassles with these buyers. They were flush with cash. Mortgages were paid off along with credit cards and any other debt they had. The 'Paid in Full' ink stamps at the banks were worn out by the end of the day.

Bob Kramer drove straight to the hardware store and bought a new chainsaw and a dog bed for his aging hunting dog, Scout. As an afterthought, he bought his wife a new turquoise bowling ball with her name engraved on it. That was a splurge for Bob. His wife had other plans for herself and made no bones about it. She went house shopping with one of the few available realtors in the valley who wasn't out showing properties. The old double-wide would be a thing of the past for the Kramers.

The Blue Moon was prepared for the night to come. They would take a 'zero tolerance' stand on fighting, and the four uniformed off-duty officers would be there to help the four bouncers. The show of force would set the tone for the evening and preserve the peace. Charlotte looked like General Patton before the troops as she laid down the law to her bartenders and waitresses. Tips would be good that night. Nobody wanted to close down early.

The pickup trucks driving along Highway 40 toward Hungry Horse were filled with big-screen TVs, refrigerators, pool tables, Jacuzzis, pianos, furniture, toys for the kids and whatever else would fit. The rest were towing new boats, campers, jet skis and snowmobiles. It didn't matter that it was summer; winter would be here soon enough, and those snowmobiles would come in handy then.

Delivery trucks and their overworked drivers were going back and forth like bees bouncing from flower to flower. They had at least a 10-day backlog on deliveries.

More backs would be 'thrown out' that day than at any other time in the valley's history as the shopping spoils were carried into their homes.

The stocks of the stores couldn't hold out much longer. The more serious shoppers were ready to drive their new cars and trucks south to the big city of Missoula and load up with the big ticket items that had disappeared so quickly from the valley.

The salespeople who worked on commission loved their new customers; the ones on an hourly wage had less patience, and it was wearing thin. To hide their jealousy, they would make jokes about their lack of taste and style. Almost everyone who didn't participate in the profit-sharing tried to bolster their spirits by ridiculing the ones who did. To them, they were the 'ugly Americans' in their own country.

As evening approached, the restaurants were preparing for the invading army from Hungry Horse. Some would taste French champagne for the first time. No beer tonight. The servers would get a kick out of watching them eat the things that they would be recommending. Escargot seemed to be the consensus. That would supply them with some wholesome entertainment.

The escapades of the workers would be fodder for decades of good stories. Johnny Carson had been including them in his opening monologue since the news was broken over three weeks ago. The newspaper cartoons were having fun with it, and 'Doonesbury' had an ongoing strip in hundreds of papers across the country that featured the hapless millionaires and their imagined 'tribulations.' To comedians and entertainers, this was just too good … and way too easy.

Cash or Charge?

The economic impact on the valley was enormous. More than one thousand checks were deposited into the local banks. Fourteen checks were lost, representing over $25 million in profit-sharing money. They would be replaced easily enough. It wasn't like losing a lottery ticket, but you never would have thought so if you had seen some of them frantically searching for their checks like it was cash left on a bus bench. Stop payments were issued, and replacements were in their hands by Tuesday.

Of those who didn't lose their checks, the tally of the shopping spree was dramatic. The employees of the Glacier Mining Company traveled far and wide to buy all they wanted. The effects of the new buying power were a force that was felt the most in Montana but reached the surrounding states. Many made the four-and-a-half-hour drive up to Calgary, Canada, in search of their material pleasures. When the first weekend finally came to a conclusion, over $400 million dollars had been spent on the following:

912 cars and trucks

237 recreational vehicles and campers

282 motorcycles

296 mortgages retired

19 foreclosures averted

31 judgments paid

323 boats

213 tracts of land (mostly waterfront)

356 homes (32 for children and 21 for parents)

59 hunting cabins

523 big-screen televisions

625 VCRs

385 satellite dishes

845 stereo systems

267 CB radios

145 pianos and organs

398 snowmobiles

543 jet skis

1,143 guns and hunting firearms

373,000 rounds of ammunition

93 fly fishing rods

832 spin casting rods and reels

236 hunting dogs

273 horses

26 ponies

81 horse trailers

145 saddles

2,354 pieces of furniture

11,300 square yards of carpeting

236 pieces of 'artwork'

626 mattresses

159 Jacuzzis

1,874 bicycles

234 backyard swing sets and slides

4,674 children's toys

112 fur coats

3,569 pieces of jewelry

632 watches

10,564 items of clothing

5,492 pairs of shoes (including 873 pairs of cowboy boots)

489 cowboy hats

1,532 power tools

2,439 kitchen appliances

29 cosmetic surgeries

67,433 gold Krugerrands

6,334,000 shares of stock

633 cameras

173 safes

6,355 pieces of sporting goods equipment

834 airline tickets (most to Disneyland)

231 Amtrack tickets

76 Caribbean cruises

166 vacation packages (most to Las Vegas)

3,321 cases of beer

1,396 bottles of champagne

1,984 bottles of liquor

394 packages of Alka Seltzer

488 bottles of Pepto Bismal

284 packages of Tums

1,534 cigars

423 wills drawn up

64 new tattoos

54 tattoos removed

47 pairs of contact lenses

121 new hairdos

790 calculators

242 lawn tractors

497 barbecue grills

17 electric wheelchairs

423 church donations

Some of the more interesting purchases included 12 Rolls Royces, 4 Bentleys, 3 Ferraris, 30 Mercedes Benz convertibles, 2 airplanes, 1 boa constrictor, 3 toupees, a talking parrot and a Caterpillar diesel earth mover.

Most of the exotic cars would take a few days to prep and ship in. The sight of a new Rolls Royce parked outside of an old mobile home would have to wait. It would not be missed by the media, which would bestow special attention on that one.

Over $20 million was donated to over 36 local churches. The average donation was right around $45,000. Six churches received over $1 million each. The pastors were singing hallelujah with renewed enthusiasm. More would come in next Sunday when the more determined long-distance shoppers returned to the valley.

A lot of the donors felt closer to God after the collection trays passed by their pews. Some felt that the money would help them enter heaven—sort of a spiritual insurance policy. The pastors understood the fallacy of their logic, but the money was accepted anyway for the good that it could do. A few sermons on the topic of grace would need to be dusted off, revisited and updated in light of the circumstances. For the time being, cold water would not be thrown on these parishioners' generous gifts.

The Lindstroms did not join in on the hundreds of shopping excursions that took place over the weekend. Brad invited John and Michael over to his home for dinner on Saturday night. Kathleen prepared most of the meal, and Brad grilled four steaks at the barbecue. They all wanted to stay out of the fracas.

When Brad said grace before dinner, he asked that the food be blessed and that his brothers would open their minds to learning about God. He was taken by surprise when John took him up on it during an after-dinner cognac and cigar out on the back deck that overlooked the Hungry Horse River. Michael was more surprised than Brad, never having given religion much thought before and he wouldn't give it much thought tonight. Brad would need more time with Michael before he would be comfortable exploring the spiritual world.

Brad asked John to attend church with him Sunday morning and he accepted. Brad wouldn't leave it up to John to find his way there. Brad and Kathleen would pick him up at nine o'clock sharp and the three of them would walk in together.

John had attended four funerals in one week, and the messages he heard intrigued him. He thought about attending church after that, and Brad's invitation was just what he needed. Timing is everything.

The three of them talked about the wild events of the previous three weeks while Kathleen stayed in the kitchen cleaning. The smell of cigars was not one of her favorite things, and she thought it best to let the brothers have a private discussion.

They reminisced about the previous thirty years, knowing that in less than 60 days, they would enter the aluminum plant for the last time as owners. John and Michael brought up the discovery of gold and Brad's unselfish remedy for the 'problem.' They both apologized again, and Brad restated his forgiveness and happiness at their contrition and change of heart. Brad was never comfortable talking about the gold and changed the subject.

"Have you decided what you're going to do now that you're both soon to be unemployed?" Brad had never asked that question. All three had worked since grade school and they were still in pretty good shape. Retirement seemed like a cruel reward for a job well done.

"I don't know yet. I guess I'll invest the money and play the stock market." Michael enjoyed the financial markets and had been the only investment counselor that John and Brad had used, except for Rex Stack. He didn't have much enthusiasm in his pronouncement though.

"I'll find a way to get my hands dirty looking for another mother lode. I'm going to set up a consulting company and take the jobs that interest me." John enjoyed geology and the solitude of exploring for ore. "I've really missed the thrill of the hunt."

"What about you, Brad? What are you thinking about doing with the rest of your life?" Michael wondered what direction Brad would take. He was too young to retire.

"I don't know exactly what I'm going to do, but it will include Kathleen." Brad's mind returned to the pictures that he had seen on television of starving children in Africa. He and Kathleen had talked about that and several other mission ideas. He was still waiting for God to lead him into the future, but nothing had come of his prayers yet. "I'd like to get involved with a good cause. I think that Kathleen and I would be great volunteers, and with my sales ability, I would like to take a shot at fund-raising."

John looked at Michael and smiled. They would let Brad and Kathleen settle on their cause and then spring the foundation on them. How could they refuse? That would be a great day!

John and Michael had never married, and the secret of the gold and the fear of sharing it kept them both bachelors. John was the poster child for loners, but Michael grew sad at the thought of dying alone. He had a string of relationships over the years, but no one had ever competed successfully with the gold and money for his attention.

John's relationships, if that's what you could call them, had been more like a sailor on weekend leave than a search for a mate. John was hopeless, but Michael had potential.

Soon, there would be no office to go to on a daily basis, and he would become a certified recluse if he didn't start socializing a little.

Kathleen emerged from the kitchen with her own glass of cognac and stood upwind of the cigar smoke. "Cheers."

She toasted her husband and two brothers-in-law. "What did I miss?"

"Not much, except that nobody is ready for retirement yet." Michael looked at Kathleen after speaking and wondered if he could find his own soul mate one day.

It was still early, but John and Michael wanted to get home and off the road before the millionaire celebrants started flitting from one party to another in their new cars and trucks.

Saint John

It was 9 o'clock, and Brad was at John's door as promised. John was dressed in a dark blue suit and had his briefcase in hand, ready to go. Brad broke out laughing. "Take off the suit coat and tie and lose the briefcase. We're not negotiating with God—we're going to learn about him."

"I didn't know what to wear. Everybody that owned a suit wore it to the funerals a few weeks ago." John was laughing again.

"What was the briefcase for?" Brad was trying to contain himself. "You looked like a Jehovah's Witness."

"I thought that I might need to take notes or something. I don't know why I had it. Maybe it was my security blanket. Gimme a break, I'm new at this."

Brad went to the car and waited with Kathleen as John took off his coat and tie and put them back in the closet. She saw the whole thing but was confused by the work clothes and briefcase. When Brad told her what transpired, she began to laugh but was careful to stop long before John got in the car.

"Good morning, Kathleen. Sorry to keep you waiting. I didn't pass your husband's inspection." John was smiling.

"Do I have to sing, Brad? You know I can't carry a tune."

"Don't worry John, Brad can't either and they haven't kicked him out yet." Kathleen was quick to point out one of the few things that the brothers had in common.

"People are going to think that the end of the world is near when they see you in church on a Sunday morning." Brad loved to tease.

"You're not making this any easier for me, you know. You can drop me off right here on the road if you don't stop it."

"Okay, okay. I wouldn't tease you if I didn't love you."

"How much does it cost?" John asked about the offering, but couldn't come up with the correct word for it. "How much does what cost?" Brad asked.

"You know, when they pass the trays, how much should I put in?" John felt like an outsider and wanted to be prepared. He didn't like large groups of people and felt especially uncomfortable in unknown situations. He would have an adult-size dose of both today.

"It doesn't cost anything. The members are responsible for church expenses. It's not expected of our guests."

Brad had to think back to the first time that he and Kathleen attended church. He had experienced some of the same anxieties. His first visit was complicated by Communion. When it was his pew's turn to go up to the altar and receive the bread and wine, he just sat there confused until Kathleen, who was more versed in matters of the church, noticed the confused look on his face and told him that it was okay for him to wait while she went up to receive the blessing. She explained the significance and symbolism to him later. Brad remembered feeling like an anarchist when, one by one, everyone else in the church left their seat and made the pilgrimage to the altar—everyone, that is, except him and a wheelchair-bound woman in the back row.

He didn't want John to get caught up in the ritual and let the message get away. Brad almost didn't return the next week after his first exposure to religion because he felt like a voyeur, spying on some very personal moments that he had no way of sharing with the others due to his nominal understanding of the church and all things spiritual. Kathleen had grown up in the church, and for her, the return was like a homecoming.

It took Brad years to grasp the basic doctrine of 'grace and forgiveness.' He had always done things on his terms and didn't rely on anyone else to get what he wanted. Brad approached religion with the same attitude. He would get to heaven by hard work and as a result of his own methods and skills. Brad had battled his own arrogance with the help of Kathleen, and by reading and studying the scriptures. He couldn't expect John to grasp the concept in an hour on Sunday morning.

"John, you've got to approach today like you would one of your geological expeditions. Keep an open mind. Don't let past experiences get in the way of what your heart is telling you. Don't be distracted by the landscape, because when the topsoil is scraped away, it will reveal the underlying truth. Just like anything in life, it will make sense to you if you read about it, learn about it, and practice it. If you want to find the lode, you can't just walk around the mountain kicking at the soil; you've got to dig a hole, crawl into it, and keep excavating and exploring until you find it. Maintaining that feeling of hope will keep you searching, and faith will eventually lead you to the ultimate 'mother lode.' It will be more precious than gold."

Brad was sounding like Pastor Ingraham, but with the dashboard as his pulpit and the steering wheel as his message as he drove down the road toward the church.

"Sorry for the sermon, John. Enough said."

"You're quite the allegorist. The gold was a nice touch. Touch!" John and Brad always loved a little jousting and they both were enjoying the first steps of the challenge that lay ahead.

They went in and sat in the second pew, but not before the greeters and ushers all shook their hands and welcomed them. John didn't like the location that Brad had chosen. It would have been better if they sat in the last pew and remained inconspicuous. What could he do? If they moved now, the negative connotation would be worse than staying put. John wondered if their ringside seats were a comp for his brother's generosity (Sort of like the big spenders in Vegas getting the royal treatment).

John was going to be a 'project', and he would require special handling.

The twelve minutes that lapsed before the service began seemed like an hour. Einstein's 'Theory of Relativity' made sense to John now. Time was definitely relative and this was relatively the longest twelve minutes he had ever experienced. He had been introduced to over twenty people and would never remember their names or faces. They sure smiled a lot, he thought to himself. Some had name tags on, and this would be helpful in distinguishing between the similar smiling faces.

The pastor walked up to the front and started with a 'good morning,' everyone responding in kind. John was sure he could tell which ones were really having a good morning—they were the ones who yelled it back the loudest.

These were Lutherans. Any public display about how they felt, no matter how controlled, should be considered enthusiastic and positive. Just a couple of months ago, one of the parishioners passed out during the early service. The paramedics were called in, and it took them a while to identify which member had passed out. Finally, a visiting Southern Baptist yelled out to them where the man was, and he was successfully revived with the help of prayer and smelling salts.

Pastor Ingraham made a few announcements about the upcoming events and identified several opportunities for volunteers to step up to the plate. The usual volunteers raised their hands, but the ones who never offered to help didn't. When he finished, he asked everyone to stand up and greet each other.

Not again! John thought to himself as Pastor Ingraham locked John onto his radar screen and, with the precision of a fighter pilot zeroed in on his target, his right arm extended forward.

"Welcome, John." Pastor Ingraham knew who John was and they had been introduced before a few times over the last five or six years.

"Thank you," John responded, wondering if he had a flashing light suspended over his head that identified him as a hot prospect for the membership rolls, or worse yet, the one who needed church the most.

John turned around and viewed more outstretched hands pointed in his direction. He dutifully shook them and was glad when the piano started with the first hymn …. that is until he realized that this was an audience participation 'number' and he would have to sing. He was glad that he was in the second row now, since no one was in the first pew and his singing wouldn't be heard by the others.

John listened to the various parts of the service and tried to understand the process outlined for him on the 'Order of Service' sheet that was handed to him when he first arrived. It seemed mysterious to him, like the time he was asked to join the Masons and witnessed the special handshakes and protocols. After that, he never went back.

Brad was glad that Communion wasn't on the schedule that morning. It would have pushed John over the limit.

The children's message was nice and related to the upcoming sermon. It was a story about a shepherd who lost a lamb from his flock. He left his flock and searched for the lamb until he found it and brought him safely home. This parable was about Jesus and how he cared for each of his little 'lambs' no matter how careless and silly they were to wander off. The children were pleased with the happy ending.

Scripture was read by one of the members, followed by more songs. John was amused by the modern style of music that had entrenched itself in a 2,000-year-old message.

Pastor Ingraham headed to the pulpit and began his sermon. John thought that he was looking at him during for most of his talk, and it made him feel uneasy. He was conscious even of the way he was holding his head and at what angle might suggest he was interested and understood the message. He was sure that everyone noticed the perceived 'special attention' that he believed he was garnering from the pulpit.

The sermon was basically the same as the children's message. It was put into a modern context, but the message was the same. John felt that he was talking about him and Brad. John was the lost lamb, and Brad was the shepherd.

Pastor Ingraham went on to talk about the new millionaires in the valley and pleaded with them to realize that they had received a gift from God, and as such, it was their personal responsibility to be good stewards of those gifts.

More music and singing were printed on his 'agenda' sheet, as he would call it. Next up was another prayer. The first prayer at the beginning of the service was more of a confession directed inward toward every person in the room. It was a prayer for forgiveness, and it praised God. The second prayer was for the world and all of the tragedies that were affecting different countries and cities that had witnessed attacks from wars, violent weather and earthquakes. It was then narrowed down to the United States and, finally, to the valley in an ode to the tragic events that they had all suffered over the past month. John had thought about those less fortunate than him many times.

The offering trays were circulated, and the money collected was blessed. These trays held over a million dollars in checks that were camouflaged by tiny check-sized envelopes. John threw in a hundred-dollar bill, and Kathleen placed her envelope containing her tithe along with Brad's. John wondered how much was in it and thought about Brad's 'share' of the gold that was deposited into the new foundation.

The final hymn was up next. John looked at his watch. An hour had passed by since the opening announcements. The service was shorter than he expected. He sat through a two-hour funeral three weeks earlier and thought that it was too long.

When they finished the hymn and the candles on the altar were snuffed out, John was ready to go. He had made it through his first regular church service in over 50 years (church weddings and funerals didn't count). He wasn't sure, but he thought he would be back next week.

"Let's get a cup of coffee in the 'fellowship hall' before we go home." Kathleen was headed into the room located off the sanctuary before she finished her sentence.

Brad led John in, and he dutifully followed. Brad would stick by his side until they left.

"More handshaking," John muttered under his breath. *This is getting a bit redundant,* he thought to himself.

While Brad was getting the coffee, John looked around the room and saw a corkboard titled, 'Prayer List.' He was bewildered by what he saw as he scanned the list of names. His name and Michael's was on the list, and his bewilderment then turned to anger.

"Let's go, Brad. I'm ready to leave."

John headed out the door and walked to the car. He got in the back seat and waited. John misunderstood the reason for his name being up there. Brad had put it up on the board so that others might pray for him, not condemn or look down on him. John had a thing about hypocrites, especially those in the church. He was reminded of Kim Sindacalo from another church in town. Kim always carried a Bible, thumped it at everyone, and was always ready to point a finger and recite a Scripture or two. Kim eventually filed fraudulent papers and filed them with the state in an attempt to receive a double payment from an out-of-state company, but the scheme backfired. Kim was caught. John's opinion of Christians was forever tainted by this pretender.

Brad stood there holding two cups of coffee, looking baffled. What could have happened in half a minute to cause John's strange behavior?

He looked for Kathleen and found her in the corner, talking to friends. He got her attention, and she approached.

"Where's John?" She asked.

"He stormed out of the church. I don't know what happened. Something upset him, he just said he was going and walked out."

"Let's find him and ask what happened." Kathleen said her goodbyes and followed Brad to the car. John was in the back seat, sulking.

"What happened, John?" Brad thought that the service was pretty painless today. Every now and then, Pastor Ingraham would pull the carpet out from under the congregation to shake the worshipers out of their complacency, like the time he dressed up as a homeless man and sat out on the steps leading up to the church entrance on a sunny Sunday morning. He wore a beard, a hat, and a ratty trench coat. He did a great job of concealing himself and at the same time, portraying one of the railroad bums that were seen from time to time wandering through the small town.

Nobody stopped even to talk to him, let alone invite this lost soul into the church for the Sunday service. Not one of the members made any effort to find out about this poor man on the steps of their church. When the pastor hadn't shown up to start the morning procession, people thought that he had slept in. Frantic calls were made to his home, but no one answered. After about ten minutes, Pastor Ingraham got up from the steps, walked into the church, and kept going up the aisle until he reached the pulpit. The little old Scandinavian ladies were horrified and looked at their husbands as if they should be doing something to stop this bum.

Pastor Ingraham took off the hat, wig and beard. As he removed the trench coat that revealed his clergy collar and robe, the worshipers laughed at the joke that had been played on them. Pastor Ingraham was in no mood for jokes and curtly announced that the sermon's message centered on Colossians 3:11-14. He would teach them about loving all people and accepting even the lowest in our society. It was such a stinging message that some of the fringes of the church weren't seen again. A hands-on church experience was a bit out of their comfort zones.

Brad couldn't imagine that today's message had anything in it that would be offensive to John.

"I want my name off that 'Prayer List.' Who do you all think you are, anyway? I may be your idea of a 'little lost lamb,' but I think that it's insulting. It's like your church is singling me out for a special project. It's embarrassing and arrogant. I don't need your prayers! What did you do? Did you consult with Ingraham about the topic of the sermon after I said that I would be coming to church with you today?"

John always got to the point quickly. Brad was smart enough just to apologize and shut his mouth.

"I'm sorry John, I'll remove your name from the list today, I wasn't thinking when I put it up there. Please forgive me."

Ouch. 'Please forgive me,' reminded John when he had asked Brad to forgive him many times during the last three weeks. Brad did so immediately, without holding back or playing head games.

Every squeak and engine noise in Brad's Lincoln could be heard above the dead silence of the passenger compartment. No one said a word. Kathleen was frozen still like a statue in a snowstorm.

"I forgive you, okay?" The noisy silence was broken by John's announcement and the two sighs of relief from the front seat.

"Thanks, John. Let's go out for brunch. I'm buying." Brad was an expert at changing the subject.

"I'm the one with all the money, I'll buy." John left his anger two blocks behind and was joking again.

"I'll buy. In case you forgot, I've got a million bucks burning a hole in my purse." Kathleen was a millionaire in her own right now, but everyone seemed to ignore it.

They drove to the Bison Cafe and had brunch. Their meal was interrupted by all the people coming over to talk about the gold and the millionaires. When the check came, John and Kathleen didn't have enough cash. Brad was the only one with money at their table. The waitress was amused by the sight of multi-millionaires trying to raise enough cash between them to buy breakfast.

"I'm out with two deadbeats." Brad took out $20 and gave it to the cashier. He left a big tip while shaking his head in mock disgust.

They dropped John off at his home, and Brad apologized again. "Will we see you next Sunday?"

"You just might." John wasn't sure. "Don't forget to take my name down."

Brad would remove it. He felt better about John's prospects for the future. He would leave Michael's up for the time being.

The Search

The weeks passed by without any major problems surfacing at the plant or in the community. John hadn't returned to Brad's church, but insisted that he was reading and learning about the church. Brad gave him a few books to read, but wasn't convinced that he had read them. John actually had read them and a few more books about Christianity that he bought himself. Kathleen had bought him a Bible, but didn't know if he had read any of it. Brad wanted to put his name back on the prayer list but decided against that.

John was traveling all over the country now in search of a consulting contract that would revive his dormant geological skills. It was a boring and dull process. Nothing excited him yet. He was a famous man in the mining industry now, known around the world for finding the largest gold vein in history. Everyone wanted him to find the next one for them, but he didn't seem to connect with anyone yet.

It was on one of those trips that he picked up a Gideon Bible that was in the nightstand of his hotel room. He started reading the New Testament and was captivated by the stories and eyewitness accounts of Christ's last three years on earth. He finished the New Testament in a week. He had started to attend church the second week after going with Brad and Kathleen; not in the valley, but while traveling. Brad thought it strange that John was never in town on Sundays anymore. Maybe he was avoiding the whole issue by not being around to decline another invitation.

He put up with the 'hostile' welcomes, smiles and hand-shakes' as he called them, and soon realized that they were motivated by the genuine care and not some phony recruitment ploy that he had once thought to be the case. He started taking Communion with the other members of the various churches that he attended. Seven weeks after Brad and Kathleen had brought him through the doors of the Christ Lutheran Church in Whitefish Lake, John was baptized during a church picnic on a lake in a small mining town in Colorado that he was visiting for his consulting business.

He learned about the picnic and the baptismal ceremony that would take place in the lake while listening to the church announcements at the beginning of the Sunday services. This was the sixth Sunday that he had gone to church, and this was the sixth church that he had been to in seven weeks. The public baptism intrigued him, and he wanted to see it for himself. He explained to the pastor that he was visiting the area on a business trip and asked him if he could attend the picnic and watch the baptism.

"Of course you may. Wait here, and I'll get you the directions."

John waited patiently as Pastor Talbot finished shaking hands with the worshippers. He smiled at John after he had thoroughly shaken each hand, and motioned him to follow him into his office to get the map.

"Where are you from?" He asked John.

"Hungry Horse, Montana." It came out of his mouth before he could stop it. John didn't like the notoriety that those three words had brought him each time he uttered them and was caught off guard by the pastor's innocent question.

"That's the town with all of the millionaires, isn't it?

"That's the one all right, and yes, I'm one of them." John beat him to the next obligatory question. He seemed ashamed somehow for being wealthy.

"Pleasure to meet you, I'm Pastor Talbot, and you're my first millionaire."

John laughed at his sense of humor. "I'm John Lindstrom, the pleasure is mine."

"Here's the map. I hope to see you there. Have you been baptized?"

"Not yet." John left with the map and walked out of the church. He would be getting wet this afternoon at the church picnic.

When he got to his car, he realized that he had let the cat out of the bag. The secret that he revealed wasn't about him being baptized; it was about the large donation that he left on the collection plate. Until now, the six churches that he visited didn't have a clue who this mysterious J. Lindstrom was that was leaving behind the big checks in the offering plates. The sole clue on the checks was that it was somebody named J. Lindstrom, and the money was drawn from the Morgan Guaranty Bank in New York City. The only thing on his check was his name. No address was imprinted on it because of the publicity surrounding Hungry Horse. Most thought that he must have been from New York.

The first check he left was to help a small church in Arizona pay off their mortgage. When he walked in the door, he noticed an easel that tallied the results of their "Move the Mountain" campaign to pay down the balance on the loan for their church building. One week was left in the two-month fundraiser, and so far, they had collected $6,000 toward paying off the $112,000 mortgage. The graph looked pitiful, with only about an inch colored in on an eighteen-inch tall 'mountain."

John left a check in the offering that day for $106,000.

He really enjoyed giving them the money. It was much more rewarding than spending it on something for himself. John was a changed man. He wished that he could have been there when the collection was added up that Sunday. He would have loved to have seen the expression on the pastor's face when he was shown the check that had the words 'Move the Mountain' in the memo line on the bottom. After he left the town, he wished that he had left more.

From that Sunday on, he was leaving a check in each of the churches' offering trays for $500,000. Most thought that it was a cruel prank until they either deposited the check and saw that it had cleared or called the bank in New York to verify the authenticity. One of the churches in Nevada removed it from the other donations and set it aside. It wasn't until the bookkeeper saw it four days later and decided to call the bank on what she called a 'lark' that it was determined to be genuine.

John had left his mark in six churches in six weeks. He had left over $2.5 million behind and relished the thought of the next one. Pastor Talbot would be the only one who knew his name and where he was from. John decided to go back into the church and ask Pastor Talbot to keep it a secret.

"Pastor, can you keep a secret?" That statement usually preceded a confession of some sort. Most were pretty tame from the people that he knew. The ones from strangers were more likely to contain a disclosure about one of the bigger violations of the Ten Commandments.

"I sure can, John. Tell me about it, and please call me Rich." John didn't miss the irony of the name. The pastor was Rich, and now, so was his church.

It wasn't what Rich anticipated. John explained that he had left a large donation in the offering tray and that he had been doing it for the last six weeks in six different towns.

He went on to say that they had all been left without any fanfare or recognition and that he preferred it that way.

"I realized that you might not be the first one to connect a face with it, but you were definitely the first one to know where the donor lives. I don't want to receive any accolades for it. That's not why I do it." John was uncomfortable even talking about it.

"Don't worry, I'm the bookkeeper, janitor, and yardman along with my other duties here. The donations are in the safe and I won't get around to depositing them until tomorrow afternoon. Your secret's safe with me."

"Do me a favor then. Don't open the envelopes until after the picnic today."

"I promise." Pastor Talbot was definitely curious about John's gift, but he was true to his word.

He figured it might be as much as $5,000. They sure could use it. He was off by two extra zeroes.

He asked Rich if he would baptize him in the lake with the others.

"Nothing would make me happier, John. When did you accept Christ into your life?"

"It's been slowly happening over the last seven weeks. I can't tell you that a lightning bolt came down or anything dramatic like that. I know that it all happened pretty quickly, but I assure you that my decision to be baptized was not without much prayer and thought. I do know that I have unconditionally accepted Jesus, and I would be honored if you would baptize me today."

These were the days that made up for all of the sad funerals and personal tragedies that constantly tested most ministers' faith. Four worshippers and one visitor from Montana had made a glorious personal decision that would culminate in a lakeside baptism.

"Let's pray over your new commitment, John."

The two traded prayers for over twenty minutes. Rich was impressed with John's prayers and was put at ease by his intelligence and grasp of the Bible's sometimes elusive message. Most new converts didn't exhibit John's spiritual maturity.

"Tell me about your family. Are you married?"

"No, I never was. I guess I'm not the type. I have two brothers and a wonderful sister-in-law back in Montana. My brother Brad and his wife Kathleen are very religious, and they started me on the path that led me to be baptized. They don't even know that I have accepted Christ yet. They worry about my soul. Boy are they going to be shocked." John wished that they could be with him today.

"I leave in the morning for Montana. They'll be the first to know. I owe them both a great debt for putting me on the right path—one that's eluded me for over 50 years. I love them both very much." John was ashamed of his past. He knew that his greed had completely overtaken his sensibilities and that the gold had become his idol. He had been on the edge of a cliff and was pulled to safety by his baby brother.

"Come on, we have a picnic and a baptism to attend. We don't want to be late!"

John followed Rich to the lake and enjoyed the food and fellowship. When the time came for the baptism, he took off his shoes and joined the other four. They all had bathing suits under their street clothes, and although it seemed that John's decision was more spontaneous, the truth was that he had given it more thought than any of them.

He felt like a new man, and he now understood what 'born again' meant firsthand. He said goodbye to Rich and his new friends and was looking forward to the solitude of his motel room. He wondered how he would tell Brad and Kathleen. He was excited about springing this surprise on them. For the first time in his life, John was not just happy but full of joy and peace. John was on fire!

He thought of calling them right away, but he wanted to see the look on their faces when they told them in person.

John would never get that chance. His plane would stall on takeoff from the small mountain airport that serviced the mining community. John would be killed along with seven other passengers and the pilot in the morning.

Another Test of Faith

Pastor Talbot heard the news as he was just sitting down to count the offerings and prepare the deposit. A call from his wife interrupted his work. As soon as he heard the news, he surmised that John was on the plane. He looked through the envelopes and money that was dumped on his desk to find the donation that John had left. He opened the plain, white letter-sized envelope that seemed out of place. Inside he found a check in the amount of $500,000, and he broke into tears. Not because of the money that John had left behind, but because of the man that he was and the impression that he had left on Rich. His generous donation was just part of the package.

Rich knew that he should be happy that John was in the arms of God. He was a minister, after all, and meeting your maker was the great reward. Rich would miss the enigmatic stranger with whom he he had spent less than five hours, yet would remember for the rest of his life. He prayed for the families of those who had died in the crash. He remembered the names of his brother, Brad, and his wife, Kathleen, and prayed for them.

Maybe he was jumping to conclusions. He wasn't sure that John was on the plane that crashed. Maybe he took another flight or changed his plans altogether. Rich jumped up from his chair and quickly put the donations that were strewn over his desk into the small safe and drove to the airport.

He went to the small commuter plane's departure gate and found Officer Jerry Braddock talking with a representative from the airline. Jerry was a member of his church and had been at the picnic the day before. Jerry saw Pastor Talbot and approached him.

"Tell me what happened, Jerry."

"We don't have all the facts yet. This will be investigated by the feds. It will take time to piece things back together. Eyewitnesses said that the plane had taken off and began a turn when it just fell from the sky and crashed. There are no survivors. The victims were all from the Denver area except for one man from Montana."

Rich asked the question that he dreaded. "Was his name John Lindstrom?"

Jerry glanced down at the list he had just received from the airline. "Yes. Did you know him?" They both knew him. Jerry had met him yesterday at the picnic; he just hadn't connected the name.

"You met him, Jerry. He was the fellow that was baptized in his clothes yesterday at the picnic. He was on his way home."

"Did you know him well, Rich?"

"I only knew him for five hours … but yes, I think that I knew him well."

"I have his home address here if you want to contact his family." Jerry wouldn't mind passing off that task to a professional.

"He only has two brothers and a sister-in-law. I have one brother's name. I'll call him." Rich wanted to learn more about him.

He drove back to his church and entered his office to track down Brad and Kathleen. He found a listing from information for a Brad Lindstrom in Hungry Horse. He dialed the number, and since it was Brad's original phone number before he added the non-published one, the answering machine picked it up. Rich left a message simply stating that he was a friend of John's and had spent the last Sunday with him in Colorado and that it was imperative that he return the call. He left both his home and church numbers.

Next of Kin

The Denver newspaper had the passenger list an hour after the crash. Hungry Horse, Montana, was recognized immediately. Within minutes, John Lindstrom, one of the owners of the Glacier Mining Company and the geologist who discovered the gold, was identified. The news wires picked it up and daytime programming was interrupted by a news bulletin and a picture of John, identified as an air crash victim in the small town of Granite, Colorado.

Brad was in his office for the last week before the sale of the plant was scheduled to go through. A call came in from Henry Peyton and Brad took it.

"Henry, how you doing? You getting ready to close and collect your fees?" Brad loved to annoy attorneys.

"Brad, you haven't heard the news? Henry didn't expect to be the one to break the news of the tragedy.

"What news? Are the buyers calling off the deal?" Henry dreaded the next sentence that would come from his lips.

"Brad, I'm sorry. I just heard on the news that your brother John was killed in a plane crash in Colorado. I thought that you knew."

"What?" Brad sat down at his desk in disbelief. He knew that his brother had left last Wednesday for Colorado to check on a consulting opportunity. He hadn't taken the company plane because he was on personal business.

"I'm sorry, Brad, I thought that you knew." Henry didn't have any details other than what he'd heard on the radio.

Nine people were dead following takeoff. "Is there anything that I can do for you Brad, anything?"

"No Henry, thank you for calling me. I've got to hang up now."

Brad set down the receiver and burst into tears. He picked up the phone again and called Kathleen. He didn't want her to find out from the television or radio. It would be better if it came from Brad. He dialed his home and Kathleen picked up the phone. She was crying.

"Oh Brad, I can't believe it. John is dead. It was just shown on television. I'm so sorry."

"I'm on my way home right now. I'll call Michael before I leave." Brad broke down again and was barely able to talk. "I love you, Kathleen."

He hung up and called Michael's office, but he wasn't in. As he walked up to Margie, he saw that she was crying. This triggered Brad again and the two of them hugged and cried together.

"I'm so sorry Mr. Lindstrom, I'm so sorry."

"Thank you, Margie. I've got to find Michael; do you know where he went?"

"He said that he was going down to the main production building. He left about five minutes ago."

Brad ran down to the plant and found Michael joking around with two of the foremen. Michael saw him running toward him and knew something serious had happened. Just like Brad, his first instinct was that the plant sale had collapsed. He would have traded that scenario for the one that Brad would tell him.

When Brad got closer, he saw the tears and ran to him, leaving the two foremen in mid-sentence. "What's wrong, Brad? What happened?"

"John was killed in a plane crash in Colorado this morning. It was on the news." Brad started to cry again and Michael put his arms around him as if to prevent him from collapsing.

"Let's get out of here. I'll take you home. Does Kathleen know yet?"

"Yes, she heard it on the television about 10 minutes ago. She's a mess."

Michael walked Brad back to the office building and out to his car. He noticed that everything had stopped and the employees were crying and offering their condolences as they worked their way through the building and out the front door. Michael opened the front door of his car for Brad and helped him in. He quickly got in and headed out of the parking lot past a tear-stained Tom.

As Michael drove Brad home, they heard on the radio the same brusque facts—nothing more than they already knew.

Michael pulled into Brad's driveway and Kathleen rushed out to share her shock and pain with John's two brothers. Brad hugged her and the three of them walked up the stairs to the house.

They went into the living room and Brad sat down in his favorite chair and started to sob uncontrollably. Kathleen and Michael left him alone.

Kathleen asked Michael to find out what had happened and to take charge of getting the complete details. They both looked over at Brad. He wouldn't be able to do anything for a while. Michael went into the kitchen to use the phone and Kathleen sat next to Brad in the big reclining chair. He rubbed his eyes and spoke.

"If only I had been more persuasive with John. He was so close to being saved and now I have only myself to blame for his fate. My big brother is dead and I'm afraid that he is in a place that I don't want to think about. I can't live with that thought."

Kathleen tried to think of something to console her husband. "You don't know where John was spiritually when he died. He always 'zigged' when everybody thought he would 'zag'." She shared Brad's concern for John's soul, but felt that she had to offer some hope nonetheless.

The phone line connected to the answering machine was ringing off the hook. "Is there a way to shut off the ringer on that phone?"

Michael quickly moved to shut it off.

"I don't have anything new except that the crash occurred in a small mining town called Granite. I phoned the police department and confirmed that John was on the plane. They will call me back to make arrangements for us to take his body home. As part of their investigation, they want someone to identify John. I'll do it. I'll use the company plane and go down to Colorado and bring John home. I already called the pilot and he will be at the airport in thirty minutes. The plane is being fueled and checked out now, so it shouldn't be more than an hour."

Michael heard them talking earlier about John's soul, and it made him think about the prospects for his own eternity. He quickly dispelled those notions. He was glad that he would be kept busy with all of the details. He wasn't good at dealing with emotional or spiritual situations.

The unlisted phone rang, and Michael answered it. It was Pastor Ingraham. He just heard the news. Michael explained that they were waiting for a call from the police so they could bring John's body home. Brad said that he would call him back after that, and Michael relayed the message.

The phone rang again, and it was the Granite Police. Michael made arrangements to meet with them in four hours at the airport. The only funeral home in the county would have John's body ready for his final trip home to Hungry Horse by the following day. Michael would stay the night and leave the next day with his brother's body on the plane.

Kathleen noticed that the answering machine's tape was full and replaced it with a new one. She was in no mood to check the messages at the moment. The one from Pastor Talbot would have brought both of them great comfort in their time of great sorrow. For now, it was tucked away in the drawer.

"I'm running home and getting a change of clothes, and then I'll be off to the airport. I'll call you when I get to Colorado."

"Thanks, Michael, I can go with you if you need me." Brad was in no shape to go anywhere.

"You stay with Kathleen and make the arrangements for John's funeral. I'll bring him home."

Michael left and the two sat back in Brad's chair and started to cry all over again.

Coming Home

Michael's plane circled the tiny airport for the landing. The remains of the airplane that killed John was still there and visible. Michael broke down for the first time when he saw it. He loved his big brother and would miss him dearly. The reality of the accident and John's death was undeniable now that he had actually seen the crumpled commuter plane.

The plane landed and taxied to the general aviation area of the airport. Officer Jerry Braddock was waiting on the tarmac and walked toward the plane as Michael was disembarking. The two spoke on the asphalt apron between the building and the taxiway. Jerry suggested that they go to the funeral home and have Michael identify his brother. Michael told the pilot to take their things to the motel, which was just yesterday, John's quarters.

Jerry and Michael left for the funeral home in a Granite Police patrol car. Michael was silent for most of the trip. Jerry was uncomfortable and decided to try to start a conversation.

"I met your brother yesterday, Michael. He attended our church picnic."

Michael was surprised and asked Jerry if he was sure about that.

"Yes. He was baptized shortly after the picnic with four others from our church. I didn't speak with him for long, but he sure impressed our Pastor."

Michael couldn't believe what he was hearing. John, the agnostic, was baptized in Granite 18 hours before he was killed. What John may have lacked in religious acumen would be offset by the 'style points' he had earned. He would have to call Brad right away. It would certainly ease Brad and Kathleen's pain. For some reason, it helped Michael. He couldn't explain why, though.

"I would like to meet with your Pastor before I leave tomorrow. Could you get me his number?"

"No need to; he's meeting us at the funeral home. You can talk with him then."

The building looked more like a house than a funeral home. It was very small and was overshadowed by the nine caskets.

Michael followed Jerry into a back room that held John's casket. The cover was opened, and Michael saw that it was John. He had what looked like a smile on his face. He was in much better shape than Michael had expected. He saw only his face, but it wasn't even bruised. John's neck was broken from the impact. There was no fire, even though the plane was fully fueled upon take off.

"You can close it now. It's John."

Pastor Talbot entered the room and asked Michael if he could be of any assistance. Michael said no and thanked him for coming. He did have some questions, however.

"Pastor, Jerry here told me that he attended your church yesterday and was baptized."

"Yes." He paused before continuing. "Are you Brad?"

"No, I'm sorry. Excuse my bad manners. I'm his other brother, Michael. Brad was too distraught to make the trip down here."

"I called him this morning and left a message on his answering machine. I need to talk to you and Brad about John's last day. Would you mind coming over to my house? My wife and I would like you to stay for dinner."

"I'll come over, but I can't stay for dinner. My pilot's over at the motel, and I should get back there." Michael wasn't ready to have dinner with a minister—especially one that he didn't know. He did want to call Brad as soon as possible.

"Whatever you wish, Michael. Your pilot is more than welcome to join us." Michael was Rich's second millionaire in two days. He was certainly different than John. He seemed to be all business.

They left, and Rich drove him to his house in his 15-year-old pickup truck. "Sorry for the vehicle. My trusty old Buick let me down last week."

As they drove, Rich told him about his five hours with John the day before. He told him about his decision to be baptized and about the half-million that he left in the collection plate. Michael was astounded. It was like his brother had a secret life that no one in Hungry Horse knew about. He told him about the other five churches that he had visited since going to church with his brother, Brad, seven weeks earlier, and he told him about the millions that he had been donating.

"He never told us any of this. His brother, Brad, is sitting at home thinking that John is burning in hell, and you tell me that the Pearly Gates were thrown open wide for him to enter. This is just incredible. How much longer until we get to your house? We've gotta call him immediately."

"Here it is." They went to the front, and Rich introduced his wife.

"I don't mean to be uncivil, Mrs. Talbot, but I have to phone my brother right away. I'll call collect; it's a long distance."

Rich told him to dial directly. They went into his study and shut the door. Michael punched in the number and waited impatiently for Brad to answer.

Kathleen picked up the phone and was relieved that it was Michael. She was tired from all of the consolation calls that were pouring in.

"Kathleen, get Brad on the phone, and you stay on the extension."

"He's asleep, I don't want to disturb him. He's got to get some rest."

"Wake him up, he won't want to miss this." Michael sounded excited and out of character.

"Is John alive?"

"No Kathleen, I'm sorry. It's just that I overheard you talking about John not being saved, and you ought to know that John was baptized yesterday by Pastor Talbot in Granite. I'm at his house now, and he spent yesterday with John. What he has to tell you is truly amazing."

"I'll get him!"

Brad wasn't sleeping yet. He couldn't. When Kathleen came into the room and asked him to speak with Michael, he sensed something was unusual.

Brad picked up the phone and Kathleen went downstairs to listen in on the kitchen extension.

"Brad? Michael here. I've got someone here that spent yesterday with John. I want you to hear firsthand what he just told me."

Michael handed the phone over to Rich and motioned for him to start.

"Hello Brad, I'm Rich Talbot, a pastor at the Granite Christian Church. I left a message for you this morning on your answering machine."

"Nice to speak with you, Rich. My wife, Kathleen, is also on the line. I'm sorry, but I haven't checked the messages on the machine. What's this about?"

"First, I want to offer my heartfelt condolences to you and your wife. I spent the day with your brother yesterday, and I want you to know what happened."

Rich reconstituted the day for Brad and Kathleen. He didn't leave out a thing. He started from the beginning when he first met John at the church, told him every detail of his conversations with him, and finally described his brother's baptism in a lake outside of town. Brad grew more hopeful with every word. He couldn't believe what he was being told.

"Your brother's in heaven, Brad, and you are the reason that he was baptized yesterday. You should have seen him in his street clothes, wading in. I have some pictures of him that I will bring with me when I attend his funeral. He was an inspiration to all of us. He truly humbled me."

"Rich, you don't know what this means to me and my wife." Brad had never felt such relief and joy as he did now. It seemed so strange to be so happy on the day that his brother died. "Did you say that you would attend the funeral?"

"I would be honored to attend."

"Let me make the arrangements. If you leave tomorrow, you can ride our company plane with Michael and John. If that's inconvenient, let me know and I'll arrange for another flight. Will you be traveling alone?"

"My wife would like to be there."

"Fine, there's plenty of room on the plane for both of you, or you can take a later flight. I'll get your tickets if you can't leave tomorrow. Just let me or Michael know. Don't worry about a place to stay; we'll make all the arrangements."

"Thank you, Rich, I can't wait to meet you and your wife. We haven't set a date for the funeral, but I expect that it will be on Thursday. Would you mind saying a few words for us?"

"Of course, Brad, thank you for offering, I was going to ask you if I could." John had left a permanent mark on Rich's life.

"It was a pleasure to speak with you. I'll see you soon. God bless you and Kathleen. Good-bye Brad, good-bye Kathleen."

Brad hung up the phone and ran downstairs to the kitchen. Kathleen was still in shock. He hugged and kissed her and jumped up and down.

"I've got to call Pastor Ingraham. He won't believe it; he just won't believe it."

Brad happily told his pastor the whole story. He would tell it again hundreds of times over his lifetime, and it would always bring smiles to the listener and the storyteller.

Brad and Kathleen were able to eat dinner, and together, they watched the news on TV about the crash and John. The pictures from the crash site were depressing, but they watched the entire segment.

"Honey, I'm exhausted; I've got to get some sleep. I've never been so volatile emotionally. I feel like I ran 100 miles."

Brad went upstairs and collapsed. He wouldn't wake up until 8:00 the next morning. He slept like a rock … his conscience was clear. If he remained faithful, he knew that he would see John again someday.

Remembering John

Michael brought John home on Wednesday morning. Pastor Rich and his wife were on the flight. The wreckage had been moved to the airport hangar to await the federal investigation. It would take a year to examine the plane, and the cause was ultimately determined to be a malfunctioning aileron flap that had turned the plane to the left during takeoff. There was nothing the pilot could do at such a low altitude to correct it before the plane stalled.

The news of John's death was noted by the other five churches that he had endowed. The name J. Lindstrom was known by everyone in each of the churches as they tried to discover the identity of this mysterious saint. Every church council member, elder and regular attendee had tried to confirm his identity. When his name was telecast and printed in all the newspapers along with his photograph, the connection was made, and the mystery ended for all five congregations.

Four of the churches were making plans for new buildings with the extraordinary gift that John had left behind. Three were planning to name their new additions after J. Lindstrom. The intended names would now have to be altered to include the word 'memorial'.

Brad and Kathleen met the plane at the Kalispell airport. They embraced Michael and were introduced to Pastor and Mrs. Talbot. Brad walked to the back of the plane and leaned over John's casket. His big brother was finally home.

Michael drove home to get changed, and Brad and Kathleen took the Talbots with them, a guest room waiting for them.

John was transferred to a hearse and delivered to the funeral home to be prepared for the viewing between 4:00 and 8:00 o'clock.

He would have a change of clothes. Brad had gone home to get his work clothes, the same outfit that John had worn while he was exploring. John's search was over, but the clothing seemed appropriate. His 'Aussie' hat was not left behind.

"I can't tell you how happy we are to meet both of you. You'll be staying at our home. Kathleen and I want to hear about your short time with John all over again. It has given us such joy to learn about John's last weeks on Earth. I fear the beating that my faith would have suffered if John had been buried without us knowing about his last day in Granite."

"I have some pictures of the baptism," Rich responded, opening his briefcase and handing them to Kathleen.

"Look at these Brad; four people in bathing suits and John fully dressed."

Brad laughed out loud at the pictures of his brother wading into the lake and getting dunked as Rich baptized him. John looked out of place at first glance—sort of like that Sunday when he came to the door dressed in a business suit with a briefcase in hand. The look on his face said it all—he was right where he belonged. He still couldn't believe his brother had plunged into religion with such enthusiasm, especially in view of that first Sunday he accompanied him and Kathleen to church. Brad was certain that hauling John into the church had backfired on them. He wouldn't even talk about it with them.

"I told Michael when I first met him that your brother was on fire. There's no telling what he could have done if God had chosen to keep him with us a while longer."

It was as if he were talking about someone else. It was such a shock to Brad that his brother was inspiring clergy after such a shaky and inauspicious beginning. Michael called this his 'secret life'.

Unlike most people with secret lives, this one was pure, innocent, and inspirational.

They arrived at the house. Brad looked at his home with a different eye. He had a pastor staying with him now. He wondered if the alcohol in the wet bar would be offensive. Maybe he should have put out a Bible or two strategically placed. Would the caffeine in his morning coffee be somehow nefarious? He laughed at the absurdity. He wasn't having God over to the house for a stay; he was having another human being, just like him. Rich wasn't here to inspect the premises; he was there because of John.

Kathleen settled them into their room, and Brad left for the funeral home. He saw Pastor Ingraham there and was told that two of the churches that John had touched during his seven-week 'walk' had contacted him and were sending their pastors to attend the services tomorrow. They asked to speak at the funeral, and Pastor Ingraham said yes, pending Brad's approval. Neither pastor had known what their benefactor had even looked like until they saw John's picture on the news. Now, they would be speaking at John's funeral.

"Of course, they may speak!" It just kept getting better. The 'faith testing' of his brother's death earlier in the week was being replaced with a faith-building lesson that had 'God' written all over it.

Brad went in to look at his brother and saw his peaceful face, and yes, he detected the smile that Michael had described to him over the phone from Granite. The expression on John's face would be burnt into Brad's mind forever.

Pastor Ingraham suggested that the services should be held in the auditorium of the mining company. "I don't think that we're going to have enough room in our church. We can only hold about 200 people, and that would be crowded."

"I think you're right, especially considering the turnout from the employees that we should expect. I'll get working on that." Brad asked him to get an announcement in the morning paper posting the changes.

They left the funeral home to work on the arrangements. Brad stopped by the office and enlisted Margie's help getting the auditorium set up for the services on Thursday. The plant would be operational in the morning but would shut down at noon. The services would be held at 2:00 o'clock.

He drove back home to change for the viewing, and he and Kathleen left for the funeral home at 3:30. They gave Pastor Talbot the keys to Kathleen's car and drew a map for him.

"Just let the phone ring; it's been ringing nonstop since Monday."

The Vigil

Brad walked into the room that held his brother's body. It was filled with flowers. He read the notes on them and saw that six of them were from congregations spread throughout the West. Each one was from one of John's consulting trips over the past seven weeks. He saw the one from the Granite church. There was one each from Arizona, New Mexico, Nevada, Utah and Wyoming. The pastors from Arizona and Wyoming would be attending the services tomorrow. Brad made a mental note to have someone posted at the church with printed maps to hand out to the ones that might miss the announcement.

Brad and Kathleen took up positions to the right of John's casket. It dawned on him that he should talk with John's attorney to see if his will contained any directions for the service. Maybe he wanted to be cremated or had some specific instructions. He would undoubtedly see him at the viewing and would ask him then.

By 4:00, the room was filled with over 90 mourners who had come to pay their respects. Brad thought it was ironic that almost none of them knew how much he had changed over the past few months. They would be coming to remember a man that they didn't really know at all.

There were quite a few tears to go around. None from Brad though—he was certain of his brother's fate, and it was not something to be cried over.

One by one, they came over to Brad and Kathleen to offer their condolences. Most didn't really know John that well. Some had never met him. It was for Brad's benefit that they were there.

Brad saw people that he hadn't talked to in years: Employees and friends from the valley and throughout the state had come to pay their respects. He was glad that the service was changed to the auditorium. More than 1,000 people signed the guest book at the entrance to the room. By 6:00, a line had formed in the outer room that poured into the main entrance and spilled out into the parking area.

Brad met the pastors from Arizona and Wyoming. The Wyoming group came with all twelve church council members. They piled into the church van and drove up from northern Wyoming. They wanted to know about John, the stranger who came out of nowhere and blessed their church with a small fortune.

John's attorney, Peter Hileman, came over, and Brad asked him if John's will had any specific instructions for the funeral and burial. He told him that John had modified it less than two weeks earlier, and it didn't address his burial, but said that recent changes had involved Brad, and he should be present for the reading.

By the time 8:00 rolled around, Brad and Kathleen were totally spent. They had promised to take the Talbots out to dinner. They normally would have begged off, but they wanted to hear about John's last day all over again.

They left at about 8:30, picked up their guests, and enjoyed the company. The Talbots asked so many questions about John starting from his childhood that midnight had come and gone before they knew it.

The drive home from the Whitefish Lake Restaurant was quiet. Everyone was tired and ready for bed.

Sorrow and Joy

Morning brought sunshine and warm temperatures. Not the usual 'funeral weather' that northwest Montana specializes in for overly extended periods of time. Brad was up before Kathleen's alarm went off, organizing his thoughts. He would be speaking for John and wanted to do more than the usual memorializing. John had a special story that needed to be told.

As Brad sat in his favorite chair recalling his brother's life, he was interrupted by Pastor Talbot walking through the living room. He, too, was organizing his thoughts for the service and didn't see Brad in the shadows until he was right next to him.

"Good morning, Rich. Sorry I startled you, I'm in my thinking chair. Thinking about John and thinking about what I'm going to say today."

"I'm doing the same thing, Brad." Rich stopped to talk with Brad. He lowered his voice as he continued. "You know, most folks assume that when a pastor or priest speaks from the pulpit, the words just materialize without preparation. It's like they think that the Holy Spirit just takes over, and all we have to do is move our lips. Sometimes, I wish it were that easy. I'll tell you though, there have been times when I wasn't quite prepared, and it was pretty obvious to my listeners. The only message I got from the Holy Spirit during those times was that I wasn't prepared. My lips were moving all right, but nothing of much value was coming out."

"I can relate to the value of a thorough preparation," Brad was always prepared when it came to pitching a prospective aluminum customer. The competition was too strong, and they were always lurking about to pounce on any weakness. "I hope I can do justice to my big brother's incredible testimony."

"I think you will." Rich wished that he had 50 years of knowing John to draw from. Five hours was the total amount of time that he spent with John. Five hours wasn't much time and would normally require some research with family members to make a respectable showing from the funeral pulpit. This wasn't like that at all. Rich had known John in a completely different way from his family and friends. He knew a John that no one else did. No one understood what had taken place in his life during the past six or seven weeks. John never made it home from his last trip to share his 'secret life' with his brothers and friends. He almost died with it. Rich had a great story to tell, and unlike most of the pastors that speak at funerals, he was a part of John's life and could speak about him in the 'first person' instead of the 'third'.

Rich asked if there was any coffee in the kitchen. Brad chuckled to himself and then jumped up to fix it for him. The two talked for over an hour before Kathleen entered the room.

"Hello Rich, hi honey." Kathleen was dressed and ready to cook breakfast for her guests and husband. "Is Ann awake yet?"

"We haven't seen her yet; she's probably getting dressed. I'll bring her some coffee."

"I'll start breakfast. Bacon and eggs okay? I have cereal if you want something lighter."

"Eggs will be just fine; thanks, Kathleen. We'll be down in 15 minutes."

Rich left the kitchen and went to see if Ann was awake yet. Kathleen came over and sat next to Brad and gave him a hug and kiss. "You look like you needed that, honey. How did you sleep?"

"Not too well. I've been thinking about John and what I was going to say today. You know where I was."

"Sometimes, I think you love that chair more than me."

Brad had a good idea of what he would say that day, but he still didn't feel prepared.

The four shared prayers before they left the house and drove to the auditorium. Brad was silent, and the other three respected his solitude. The reality of the funeral was hitting home. Somehow, a death doesn't seem real to most people until the actual service and burial has taken place. Brad was still in a state of denial. Everything would settle today. He was glad to see Michael pull into the plant in front of him. He needed him now.

Michael got out of his car, walked over to Brad, and put his arms around him. Michael told Brad that he loved him and needed his help to get through the day. It finally fell on Michael, and he looked like he had been up all night. The bags around his eyes were from the crying. It all came out when he got home from the funeral home. He had been putting off that moment since he first heard Brad tell him that his brother had been killed. Michael couldn't fool his mind any longer. He had hoped to pace himself so that he could make it through the service, but sometime the night before, he just ran out of the fighting energy. He couldn't keep the fences around himself electrified any longer, and the pain and sorrow of losing his brother invaded his unprotected heart. Michael was devastated.

Brad thought that maybe he could explain it from his perspective; maybe that would make his brother feel better. Michael wouldn't understand. He wouldn't try now; instead, he would use his memorial talk as a way to get through to his brother.

They all went into the auditorium. The service would be starting in half an hour. Brad wanted to stand at the entrance and receive the mourners. Michael stood next to him.

One by one, they arrived. Brad and Michael stood guard and greeted more than fifteen hundred friends, acquaintances and strangers. They saw the two church groups that John had visited in Arizona and Wyoming again. They also met the pastors and their wives from the other four churches that John had called upon while on his business trips. Each asked if they could say 'a few words'. They were directed to Pastor Ingraham to coordinate their participation. Brad was thrilled that they came to the funeral and looked forward to spending time with each of them. Maybe additional pieces of the puzzle would reveal more of the big picture.

The people from the mortuary had moved in all of the flower arrangements. The stage looked like a flower show exhibit. John's casket was on the main floor, surrounded by even more flowers. The auditorium was filled to capacity. Brad and Michael left their posts and walked to their chairs in the front row. Kathleen reached for Brad and Michael's hands as they sat on each side of her and squeezed them tight. Pastor Ingraham was ready to begin. The church piano was played by Tillie. It had been moved over the night before by her doting husband, Art, and some of the younger ones from the church. It sounded beautiful inside the huge room.

Pastor Ingraham began the service with prayer, though not for John—he was departed and beyond prayer's reach—it was for the family and the friends that John had made over the years, particularly in the last two months. Pastor Ingraham understandably never liked funerals. You could never be sure if the dearly departed were headed north or south. Some of the ones you would least expect to make it into heaven were there now, and certainly, some of the sure bets for heaven were making their restitution in the hereafter somewhere else.

John seemed to be a 'sure bet,' and that was uplifting and enlightening. The ceremony and the messages would take their cues from that assumption. The pastor took care of the church's rites and rituals before turning the lectern/pulpit over to Brad. Pastor Ingraham had barely known John and was glad that Brad bailed him out of the awkward task of memorializing someone that he didn't know. That's the hardest job for a pastor or priest. Usually, the ones you don't know are the ones who didn't attend church. Trying to say a few nice words for the dead knowing that the odds that they made it to the great reward were rather meager. The grievers would rather 'hope for the best' rather than face the cold reality. It sometimes made the whole ceremony seem totally fraudulent, but what could you do? Using fear as a tool for induction into the church was risky business and would bring despondency to the family members, some of whom were already believers. Timing is everything, as Brad was fond of saying, and this wasn't the right time for Pastor Ingraham.

Brad went up to the lectern with one note card. On it was written the topics that he wanted to talk about.

Brad looked over the mourners and after scanning the entire room, began to speak. "My brother John is in heaven. I have no doubt about that. How do I know? I'll explain that in a moment." John's conversion was virtually unknown to the residents of the valley, while his newfound religious enthusiasm was considered the norm to most of the people whom he had touched over the last few months.

"John would be surprised to see all of you here today. He was a bit of a loner. He always seemed to be in his element when he was in some dark mine exploring for mineral deposits. He became a famous person in the mining industry by finding the largest gold deposit on Earth. He made us all rich when that gold was sold, and the proceeds were divided between us." As Brad looked around the room, he noticed people nodding in agreement.

"Most of you don't know about his latest discovery. It's much more precious than gold and, unlike John's 1954 discovery, was able to bring him real happiness. That discovery could have remained a secret if my brother Michael hadn't spoken with a pastor from a small church in Granite, Colorado, where he had gone to bring John's body back home to Hungry Horse. Pastor Rich Talbot and his wife are here today and he will be speaking to you in a little bit." Rich smiled.

"John was on a journey for the last eight weeks that ended with his baptism in Colorado this last Sunday." Brad recounted the story of John's last day with Rich Talbot. He'd left some of the good parts for Rich to tell.

Brad went on to tell the parable about the workers who were paid equally. He asked those who had their Bibles with them to turn to the Book of Matthew, Chapter 20.

After reading the 16 verses, he explained that, although John had entered God's kingdom after only a few weeks of 'work', his reward would be the same as someone who had a lifetime commitment of faith. "Although some might think that John was undeserving, that it's somehow not fair, the truth is that no one is deserving of entering heaven. God's grace is a gift to all of us who believe, no matter how long or how short the duration. There is no such thing as seniority in God's eyes; the only thing that counts is sincerity." Brad was thankful that the rules for entering heaven were that simple.

"So the last will be first, and the first will be last." As Brad read the 16 verses, he understood the meaning like never before. It didn't matter how long you believed, how long you behaved, or whatever way you tried to measure your faith. The rookie was as good as the seasoned pro in the eyes of God. "This parable should be of great comfort to those of you today who feel like outsiders when it comes to religion. Give it a try, or as John might say, 'Come on in, the water's fine'." Brad couldn't help himself and looked over at Michael.

"One of the pastors here today asked me what denomination John was affiliated with. I had to laugh because John was too naïve about formal religion to make such distinctions. He wasn't a Lutheran, or a Baptist, or a Catholic. John was a Christian and felt at home in many different churches. In fact, I don't think that John was ever in the same 'brand' of church more than once, outside of a funeral or wedding." John was as innocent as a child in matters of religion; he grasped the fundamentals without all the distractions that only served to distract him.

Brad spoke about John's childhood and college years and how the three brothers got into the mining business. He talked about his recent travels and his new consulting company. He was finishing up and almost ready to turn it over to Pastor Ingraham.

"I'm not going to cry here today because I know that my brother's soul is safe." Almost as soon as he said it, he started to cry. Brad couldn't believe it and tried to stop without success. He smiled at the show of emotion.

"I guess I'm going to cry and smile at the same time. Even though John is with God, I'm still going to miss him a lot." Brad summed it all up in three words. "Sorrow and joy."

Pastor Ingraham led the choir as they sang Amazing Grace. Michael sang along while reading the words from the handouts. Brad wondered what he was thinking.

The pastor invited the visiting clergy up to the front and turned over the lectern to them. One by one, they each recalled what they knew about John. Everything that they knew had been learned after his death. They all told how John had generously endowed their humble churches with enough money to allow great works to be accomplished. Brad couldn't wait to spend time with them after the service. Most wouldn't be able to shed any light on John's final weeks, but that didn't matter. Just knowing the impact that John had left on each of the small churches was sufficient.

As Arizona was finishing, Pastor Ingraham walked up to lead the auditorium in prayer, which dovetailed nicely with Brad's message of sorrow and joy. Tillie played the final hymn as the Lindstroms escorted John out to the hearse.

The automobile procession slowly made its way to the cemetery, and then, there were a few more words and a final prayer before John was lowered into the ground. The warm sun felt good on the dark clothes.

Brad, Kathleen, Michael and the Talbots headed back to the Lutheran church for supper, as was the custom. The ladies of the church had things organized, as did any military operation. They would jump into action and always have things just right. Brad looked forward to speaking with the four other pastors. Until then, he hadn't said more than a couple of words with any of them. What he learned about John's gifts astounded him. Each of the small churches had been struggling to pay their bills. So much time was being spent on worrying about where the money would come from that the ministries were suffering. John had given them a freedom that solidified their faith and expanded their missions. He was a one-man mercenary force.

By the following day, most of the out-of-town visitors would be gone, and life would begin its slow and inevitable journey back to 'normal'. The sale of the plant was scheduled to take place on Tuesday of the next week. Brad and Michael would be retiring after more than thirty years of planning and working for the Glacier Mining Company. It wouldn't be the same without John.

Brad and Kathleen dropped the Talbots off at the train station. They were going to Spokane to visit friends before returning to Granite. Michael left the supper early and went home. Brad was glad that the two of them were alone. He thought about the day and about the impressions that his brother had left on those six churches. Brad wanted to continue in his brother's 'work'. He would find a way to raise money for small churches that were in financial trouble and give them the freedom to concentrate on their mission, instead of their bleak financial statements.

Brad and Kathleen talked about it for hours, and she thought it was a great idea. "Count me in."

They tallied up their assets, and with the sale of the plant, they would have about $70 million to work with.

"If we invested it in a reasonably decent fund, we should be able to buy down the mortgages for hundreds of churches annually without diminishing the principal." Brad was on a roll.

"Why do we have to limit it to existing churches? We could use some of it for 'seed' money to get new churches off to a good start," Kathleen added.

"Sure. Why limit ourselves? We can do whatever we want. I like the way you think, honey."

The two of them worked on spreadsheet projections and liked what they saw. Estimating an annual income of ten million, they could help hundreds of churches a year. They decided to call their new endeavor the J. Lindstrom Foundation, exactly what was printed on John's checks. It wouldn't be John Lindstrom; it would be J. Lindstrom.

It was after midnight before they thought about the time. They both headed up to bed and collapsed. Brad fell asleep as he prayed for his new calling.

The Will

Peter Hileman called Brad the next day and asked when would be a good time to go over John's legal matters, including his last will and testament. Brad asked that he put it off until after the sale of the plant on Tuesday.

"Brad, I don't think that it should wait another day. The disposition of the proceeds from the sale should be addressed now to avoid excessive tax liability. I spoke with Michael, and he said he could meet later today. It won't take more than 45 minutes. I wouldn't ask you if it wasn't important."

"Okay, how about four o'clock?"

"That's fine—and bring Kathleen; she's mentioned in the will."

Brad agreed. He found Kathleen in the yard and told her about the meeting.

"Why do I have to go?" Kathleen just wanted to stay home and work in the yard and on ideas for the new foundation.

"Peter said that you're mentioned in the will and that you should be there for the reading. Maybe John's leaving you his stuffed antelope head to put on our living room wall."

As 3:30 approached, Kathleen alerted Brad. The two cleaned up and headed over to Peter's office. Michael was already there and inside the conference room as they were shown in.

Peter entered and, after expressing his condolences once again, got down to business.

"John had a series of wills drawn up by me over the last 20 years. The last modification was executed by John less than three weeks ago. It was witnessed by me and Marylin, my secretary. Before I read that will, I have a letter from John to you, Brad. My instructions are to read the letter first. If you have no objections, I'll read it in the presence of Michael and Kathleen."

Brad nodded his head in agreement.

To My Brother Brad,

I write this letter to thank you for being my brother and for looking out for me when I was lost and needed someone with a good compass. I want to thank you for taking the heat along with Michael and me. You convinced us to share the gold with the employees of the Glacier Mining Company. You courageously refused to be a part of our plan to hide the gold and keep the profits. Michael and I both regret that we ever even considered such a thing. Without your guidance, we would probably be headed down the path to jail.

You cared enough for me to invite me into your church. I agreed because I wanted to have some of your happiness. I now have learned what you meant by having a purpose. I read the New Testament last week, and I want you and Kathleen to know that I couldn't believe what it said. It was so simple that even a skeptical scientist like me could understand. I know that I have a lot to learn, but I have accepted Christ and I have you and Kathleen to thank.

When you refused to accept your portion of the gold, even after we disclosed its existence to the mining employees, Michael and I were stunned at the depth of your character. You shamed us. We deserved it.

Michael and I decided to hold it for you. We literally flipped a coin, and I won. We agreed to put the money into a charitable foundation—The Brad & Kathleen Lindstrom Foundation. I hope that you will accept it. I am listed as the chairman of the foundation. Upon my death, it passes to you and Kathleen. I

"It's a beautiful letter, Brad." They were all touched by John's words. Brad realized that the message from God that he was waiting for over the last few years was spoken to him through his brother John's letter. He looked at Kathleen, and they both knew what direction their lives would be taking. God used a converted agnostic scientist to deliver a message to them.

"I have a letter for Michael. If it's okay with you, Michael, I'll read it now. This letter is dated less than two weeks ago."

Michael was ready and nodded in acknowledgment.

My Dear Michael:

Thank you for everything that you have done for me over the years. Sometimes, we forget to say the words that we think out loud to the ones that should hear them. I don't think that Brad would have been successful in convincing me to share the gold if you hadn't changed sides and teamed up with him. I regret that I was so stubborn and so greedy. Thank you for interjecting a little sanity back into my brain.

I really delighted to have you as my brother. We fought a lot when we were growing up, but no matter what happened, I always loved you—even when I was six years old and you put that garter snake down my back and called it a rattler.

I have a request that I want you to accept with an open mind. I want you to read the Bible and go to church with Brad and Kathleen. You'll find the answers to the hardest questions. I hope that you will give it a chance. I can't tell you the joy I have received. It's like nothing I have ever experienced.

I hope that you will help Brad and Kathleen with the foundation. They could use your financial expertise. With over $1.5 billion to work with, it should be enough to keep you interested. I hope that some of the funds will be used to support churches throughout the world.

I don't know why I am writing this letter to you or the one that I wrote to Brad a few days ago. I'm certainly not planning on dying. I just felt like it was important to put my thoughts in writing. Something is telling me to do it now and not to wait.

I love you and thank you for being my brother and friend. Listen to your baby brother every now and then. Good-bye.

The four of them sat quietly for a while. Peter had never been involved with the reading of a will of this magnitude and knew that he probably never would again. Most of his readings involved leaving a house and some cash to family members. The last one he read left a canary and a bulldog to a relative who lived in an apartment house in Missoula. The recipient had been only too glad to inform them of all of the regulations prohibiting pets of any kind. The bird is with Peter's niece, and the bulldog went to Marylin's brother in Bigfork.

Peter asked if anyone needed water or coffee. Brad asked for water, and Marylin brought out glasses on a tray with a full pitcher of ice water. Everyone decided that the water was a good idea.

"Shall we proceed?" Peter asked. "There aren't any surprises. John's letters pretty much spelled it all out." Peter picked up the six-page document and began to read it aloud.

"The Last Will and Testament of John Cody Lindstrom. I, John C. Lindstrom, a resident of Flathead County, Montana, declare that this is my will.

I revoke all wills and codicils that I have made previously.

I am a single, unmarried man.

I hereby………"

Peter read through the boilerplate of the will and got to the meat. John had left his entire fortune to Brad with a request that it be added to the foundation's deposits. He also addressed his portion from the sale of the plant and left the expected $23 million to Kathleen. His instructions were for her to use it for any purpose that she wanted.

Peter finished reading the document and asked if there were any questions.

Brad had one. "Michael, were you aware of John's latest will?"

"Yes, we talked about changing our wills the weekend that the foundation was formed. John and I didn't know what to do with 'your share' of the gold. We couldn't divide it between us. John came up with the idea of creating a new foundation and putting all the money into it. We knew that we could keep it quiet for a time, and we expected that when you found out about it that you would accept it in the spirit in which it was created."

"Peter, can we change the name of the foundation?" Brad didn't want it named after himself.

"Of course you can; it will just take a little paperwork. What do you have in mind?"

"Yesterday, Kathleen and I decided to form a foundation in John's memory. We are calling it the J. Lindstrom Foundation. The purpose was to help churches get over financial hurdles. The idea was to carry on what John was doing throughout the West, helping small, underfinanced churches free themselves from the burden of debt. You probably noticed Kathleen and I looking at each other in amazement as you read John's letter to us. The mission of our foundation and John's is identical." Brad looked at Peter and then Michael before continuing.

"I accept the position and responsibility, with the exception of the name. From now on, it will be called the J. Lindstrom Foundation."

"Brad, I need to know how you want me to direct John's gold proceeds and the other assets that total around $900 million. It's your call. If you need time to decide, just let me know as soon as you can." Peter didn't want to push him, but the tax implications for such a large fortune were enormous.

"Put all of it into the foundation!" Brad had no hesitations about that. The money would be used to do wonderful things and would continue John's short legacy. "Michael, I hope that you will help us with the foundation. We will need your help."

"I will be honored to work with the two of you. I would like to donate enough money to bring the principal amount of the foundation to $2 billion. Let me know what the amount is, and I will write a check. I think that John's generosity is contagious. He must be smiling right now."

Peter handed over papers for them to sign. They were exchanged and witnessed. Michael, Brad and Kathleen decided to get something to eat and talk about their new future together. Michael was dumbfounded at Brad and Kathleen's identical idea for the foundation. He wanted to learn more about this seemingly amazing coincidence.

The Closing

It was Tuesday, and everything was scheduled for the 2:00 o'clock closing to transfer ownership of the Glacier Mining Company. Michael and Brad had spent most of Monday packing up their offices and moving out 30 years of memories. It was hard on them both. They collected John's things and had them delivered to Michael's house for the time being.

The conference room at the office was filled with boxes of papers and attorneys milling around. Henry Peyton came in and shook hands. Henry would be pocketing close to a million dollars that day. He was in a good mood.

With all parties present, Brad took control and stood at the head of the table before the group of two dozen, 'asking' if he could say a few words. Before anyone could respond, he began to speak.

"Not all of you know me; my name is Brad Lindstrom. Today is a great day for the Glacier Mining Company. My two brothers and I worked on this project and in this plant for over 30 years. With over a thousand employees over that time, we kept this place cranking out aluminum. I will miss coming to work, and I will miss the people that work here very much. I pray that the new owners will treat the remaining workers with fairness and respect. God bless us all."

Applause broke out while Brad went over to stand by his brother Michael. He had just handed over the reins to their empire. The signing of the papers would make it official, but in his mind, it was already a done deal. His office looked strange without anything in it. If he wanted to enter the plant tomorrow, he would need a pass. It was all behind him now. He was thankful that he had a new mission to work on. He couldn't retire at his age; it would kill him.

The whole ceremony took less than 30 minutes. Brad and Michael shook hands and left the conference rooms with their checks and document copies. The checks for all of the employees that were sharing in the sale were given to Henry Peyton to distribute on Friday. They wouldn't seem like much money compared to the gold proceeds, but it was nothing to ignore.

Brad and Michael were both taking some time off, but would return within the month to work full-time at the new foundation.

The media would find out about the new J. Lindstrom Foundation when the papers were filed for the name change. They would learn more details when John's will was filed with the state and made public. The news story about this $2 billion foundation returned a shred of respectability back into the community. The news was still playing up the materialism that had gripped the valley, but most of those articles were now relegated to the tabloids that screamed the stories at you while you were waiting in the supermarket checkout lines.

In fact, most of the workers had learned to deal with all the money fairly well. Tim Mckendricks lost everything in Las Vegas and was there at the plant, begging for his old job back. He went through $2 million in 10 days and barely had enough money to take a cab to the airport to get back home. He got his old job back. He was a sobering reminder to the others.

The initial buying spree that consumed them had subsided and allowed the employees to take a breath and think about their embarrassing and shameless materialism. Money had been an idol to some of them. It would take a few serious soul-searching sessions for them to realize that happiness wouldn't be found in their toys or bank accounts.

A news network did make a television mini-series. You couldn't glean much from it other than violence and greed. Literary latitude made sure of that. It was a ratings success, according to the folks at Nielson. The name Hungry Horse, it seemed, had been permanently tainted by the media. A few books were written about the subject, and numerous doctoral theses were submitted to economics departments at universities across the country. Not much was made of the foundation's agenda. Evidently, it didn't have the right stuff for prime time.

A lot of strangers moved into the area. Most had good intentions; many didn't. Over 50 long-time residents picked up and left. Warmer climates and a lifestyle that better suited their new 'stations' drew them away to parts unknown.

Things calmed down at the schools. The pecking order was determined by the usual criteria once again. Girls with blonde hair and boys on the football team were the 'old standard'. The kids were glad to have it back; they preferred it to the 'gold standard'.

The Blue Moon was the same as ever, although it did seem a little tamer to the regulars.

Church attendance was on the rise. Having a big pile of money would always cause more unpredictable problems than having a small pile. Evidently, answers to the problems were sought through worship. The membership levels increased slightly, but it was the attendance of the old members that had increased the most.

The foundation was in high gear. Brad had Michael personally deliver some of the checks to the churches. There were just too many for one person, though. Once the foundation was up and running, they were sending out over eight checks a day to pay off mortgages or for new construction. In the first year, almost three thousand churches would be recipients of the J. Lindstrom Foundation's gifts.

Michael really enjoyed going to the church service and leaving John's Memoriam behind. Just like John had done, the money was left in the offering tray with no fanfare or recognition.

Michael became an expert on all the different denominations. He had been to so many churches over the first year that he started participating in the services with great enthusiasm. Lo and behold, Michael himself was baptized during one of his trips. On another of his church gift-giving trips, he met a woman. This was the one that he had been waiting for all his life and he told everyone as if to strike an offensive blow to those that couldn't believe that he was seriously in love. They were married six months later.

He often joked with Brad and Kathleen that he felt as if he were delivering checks for the Reader's Digest Sweepstakes winners. Brad and Kathleen often joked that Micheal was the actual winner. He had never been happier.

Thousands of requests were received from every imaginable church group. Some obvious phonies were discarded immediately, while certain denominations with histories of dubious doctrine or suspect leadership were eliminated from consideration.

When a church was selected as a potential recipient, the foundation would send in a representative to witness their Sunday service and make a general assessment of their needs. It was sort of like the food critic from a newspaper going incognito to get an accurate sampling of the fare. The purpose of the visit from the foundation wasn't to critique a church, however, but to offer help in all areas of church ministry and business. The foundation would go on to offer educational programs for new and existing churches as part of their ministry. Running a church was much more involved than most of the pastors had expected. Seminary schools often lacked business acumen.

Brad's style of leadership was a perfect match for the new foundation and the churches they served. He wasn't one for much talk. Brad, Kathleen and Michael's foundation taught by example, not by rhetoric. 'Preach the Gospel, and when necessary, use words' was the motto of the J. Lindstrom Foundation.

John would have approved.

I dedicate this story to my three wonderful children.

May they make the right decisions in their walk through life.

About the Author

JK Worth is a passionate storyteller who splits time between the majestic landscapes of Montana and the open waters of the Gulf and Atlantic. After dedicating thirty years to raising three wonderful children, JK now enjoys life aboard the family yacht, "Big Sky," cruising between Orange Beach, Alabama, the Florida Keys, and the Bahama Islands. With a deep appreciation for adventure and a rich imagination, JK channels these experiences into compelling narratives that captivate readers.

Inspiration strikes in the most unexpected places and the name of JK's beloved yacht has already sparked ideas for future works. Whether on land or sea, JK remains dedicated to crafting stories that explore the complexities of human nature, as seen in the latest novels, *The Hungry Horse* and Columbia Falls.

JK Worth can be reached at: jkworthauthor@gmail.com.